Design and Illustration
PEGGY HERING

Food Photography
JOSE MOLINA

Cooking & Cruising
Italian Style

COSTA'S LIGHT & HEALTHY CUISINE

Editor: LUCY COOPER

Surfside Publishing

Senior Editor: LUCY COOPER
Assisted by: McVAY CHRISTY
Miguel A. Seco

Illustrations and Design: PEGGY HERING
Typesetting: DAVE CLAUSSEN
Brenda Fuentes

©Copyright SURFSIDE PUBLISHING AND COSTA CRUISES, INC.
Photographs and artwork ©SURFSIDE PUBLISHING AND
COSTA CRUISES, INC.

Manufactured in the United States of America
ISBN: 0-942084-89-6
Library of Congress Catalog Number: 89-06-789

Table of Contents

Acknowledgements

Many thanks to the Costa onboard hotel personnel who contributed their beloved recipes:

Chief Purser:

Rocco Auteri
Silverio Aversano
Vittorio Buscaglia
Enzo Correale
Lorenzo Dasso
Raffaele Gualco
Giacomo Lupi
Vesno Petruccione
Alfredo Salomoni

Executive Chef:

Antonio Armocida
Mario Cabrio
Pasquale De Ceglia
Sebastian Leimgruber
Dino Pavero

Maitre D':

Vittorio Anselmi
Armando Ascione
Alberto Civitella
Giorgio Crivelli
Enzo Di Simone
Giuseppe Favretto
Emile Girault
Mario Orengo
Mario Pasin
Salvatore Salerno

And many thanks to the Costa executives who made the production of this book possible:

Bernal Quiros
President and Chief Executive Officer

Paolo Benassi
Senior Vice President

Mitchell J. Schlesinger
Senior Vice President

Martha A. Limner
Public Relations Manager

Special thanks to:

Luciano Cappelletto
Director of the Food Department of
Arbone Catering of Genoa, Italy

Photographs

Introduction

There has long been a romantic affair between cruise ships and grand cuisine, nowhere better manifested than on the sleek Italian ships that have plied the oceans in this century offering travelers a bounty of *cucina italiana* that might otherwise be found only in the finest restaurants of Rome, Milan, Florence, Genoa and Naples.

Indeed, many of the best Italian restaurants in the United States are run by those chefs, maitre d's and captains who once served on the transatlantic liners of the 1950's, an era when there were no higher standards for food and service in the world than those onboard Italian ships.

Yet for most Americans, Italian food and service evolved more out of a tradition of immigrant cookery and mom-and-pop restaurants catering to American tastes. Today, dishes such as *Veal Parmigiana, Chicken Tetrazzini, Clams Posillipo* and *Fettuccine Primavera* are really American creations, yet they are among the most popular items on most Italian-American menus. The true taste of Italian cuisine has largely been compromised by Italian-American dishes which, though delicious in their own right, do not begin to reflect the extraordinary range and quality of the traditional, classic Italian kitchen, nor display familiarity with modern concepts of cooking the way it is now done in Italy.

This begun to change in the late 1970's and early 1980's when more Northern Italian restaurants — many run by former ships' staff members — began to open in New York and other cities, and menus began to reflect a lighter, more elegant style of cooking. Dishes such as *Trenette Al Pesto, Spaghetti Alla Bolognese, Carpaccio, Bollito Misto, Tiramisu* and *Gelati* are now more available. Americans who traveled to Italy, whether on a ship or by jet, returned with a passion for the exquisite flavors of extra virgin olive oil, white truffles, mascarpone cheese and true scampi. The taste of Italian figs, prosciutto and funghi porcini was fresh in their memory. Today, one can probably find more imported Italian products on supermarket shelves than any other ethnic ingredients, and Italian restaurants, from small neighborhood trattorie to grand palaces of haute cuisine, have become not just fashionable, but the places you'll find the best traveled, most sophisticated diners in the world.

It seems fitting, then, that the recipe collection in this book should celebrate the great tradition of Italian cooking in a new era of cruise ships. Here you will find extravagant dishes such as *Giant Lobster Fra Diavolo* and *Spaghetti With Sea Urchin Sauce,* as well as dozens of simple, fresh, traditional dishes that truly express the Italian manner, like quickly cooked *Spaghetti With Ripe Tomatoes And Red Pepper,* or a hearty *Chicken, Rice and Cabbage Soup "Bella Romagna."*

There are several recipes for the irresistable puffy bread called *Focaccia,* as well as rich desserts like *Torta Cassata* and a hazelnut pudding called *Budino Al Gianduia.*

Finally, these recipes are as easily reproduced by the home cook as they are in the onboard galleys, which is, essentially, what good Italian cooking is all about—the use of the best ingredients in the simplest of ways to achieve a balance of flavors that do not interfere but truly enhance each other.

So, whether you enjoy these dishes as you cruise among exotic ports of call, or make them at home, you can be assured that they represent the authentic taste of Italian cooking as you recall them in your fondest memories of travel abroad.

John F. Mariani
12/89

John F. Mariani is Food and Travel correspondent for Esquire Magazine, Food Writer for U.S.A. Today, author of The Dictionary of American Food & Drink, co-author of The Passport Guide to New York Restuarants, Editor of Mariani's Coast to Coast Dining, and host of the PBS TV services, "CRAZY FOR FOOD".

From The Galley

Ciao!

Travel throughout Italy and you encounter the diverse variety of regional Italian cooking. From Palermo to Naples, Rome to Florence, Milan to Venice, you taste an endless bounty of culinary toasts: the spicy red sauces of Sicily, the miracles of *Florentine vitello,* and the rich flavorful pesto of Genoa are but a few of the glories of regional *cucina italiana!* Make such a journey and you will understand why living well and eating well are an inseparable love affair, part of the Italian devotion to *la dolce vita.*

In the following pages, the Costa Chefs and I invite you to join with us in a celebration of the glories of Italian cuisine by sharing our favorite regional dishes. The recipes are easy-to-prepare and beautifully presented. Many of them are handed down from generation to generation, preserving the time-honored tastes of the Costa tradition. Also, the recipes incorporate our diverse knowledge of European and American methods of cooking, thereby creating a world-class menu with a distinctively light and healthy Italian accent. *Bellissimo!* What could be closer to perfection?

Try these recipes soon: Feast your eyes and your palate! let the good life begin!

Buon appetito,

Paolo Benassi
Senior Vice-President
Hotel Operations

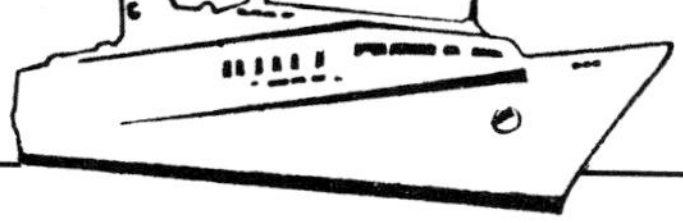

Roasted Peppers
Stewed Peppers
Marinated Ceci Beans
Garlic and Anchovy Dip
Spinach and Cheese Stuffed Eggs
Tomatoes With Tuna And Yogurt
Peas With Parma Ham
Smoked Tongue And Swiss Cheese Canapes
Stuffed Mushrooms
Marinated Mushrooms
Prosciutto And Fruits
Fondue Piedmontese
Grilled Mozzarella
Florida Oysters
Crabmeat Baked In Pastry
Potato-Cheese Croquettes
Asparagus Milanese
Eggplant Caponata

Appetizers

Roasted Peppers

(PEPERONI ARROSTITI)

4 large green bell peppers
4 large red bell peppers
¼ cup olive oil
2 tablespoons lemon juice
½ teaspoon salt

Quarter peppers lengthwise, remove stems and seeds. Arrange on broiler pan, peel side up. Broil 2 inches from heat for 10 to 15 minutes, watching carefully, until peppers are charred.

Immediately place peppers in a paper bag, close tightly and allow peppers to cool.

Peel peppers. Cut lengthwise into about ½-inch strips.

Combine oil, lemon juice and salt; mix well. Pour over peppers and toss gently. Cover and let stand at room temperature for about 1 hour, stirring occasionally.

To serve, drain peppers and arrange on platter.

Serves 4 to 6

Stewed Peppers

(PEPERONATA)

6 tablespoons olive oil
1 medium onion, chopped
2 large red peppers, cored, seeded and cut into strips
1 celery stalk with leaves, cut into 3-inch lengths, and then
into strips
4 ripe tomatoes, peeled, seeded and chopped
Salt and pepper to taste

Heat olive oil in a large saute pan. Add onion and saute until limp, then add the peppers and celery. Saute for 2 minutes. Add tomatoes, turn down heat to a simmer, and simmer slowly until vegetables are cooked and liquid reduced, about 30 minutes. Season with salt and pepper and serve hot or cold.

Serves 4

Marinated Ceci Beans

(INSALATA DI CECI)

2 (15-ounce) cans garbanzo beans
1 clove garlic, minced
½ teaspoon dried rosemary, crushed
1 cup water
¼ cup olive oil
2 teaspoons salt
⅛ teaspoon pepper

In a saucepan, combine undrained beans, garlic, rosemary and one cup water. Bring to boil, reduce heat, cover and simmer for 15 minutes. Drain well.

In a screw-top jar combine oil, vinegar, salt and pepper. Cover and shake well. Pour over beans, and toss to coat beans well. Cover and refrigerate several hours or overnight, stirring occasionally.

To serve, drain beans and use as part of an antipasto tray.

Serves 4 to 6

Garlic And Anchovy Dip
(BAGNA CAUDA)

¾ cup butter or margarine
⅓ cup olive oil
6 to 8 anchovy fillets, chopped
2 cloves garlic, minced
Assorted vegetable dippers: asparagus, carrots, cauliflower,
   celery, radishes, green peppers, mushrooms, cubed Italian bread

In a saucepan heat butter or margarine with olive oil. Add ancho-vy fillets and garlic. Cook over low heat, stirring constantly, until anchovies dissolve into a paste (the solids will separate from the clear butter and oil mixture).

Transfer to a small fondue pot and place over burner. Dip raw vegetables and bread slices into the hot mixture.

Serves 6

Spinach And Cheese Stuffed Eggs

(UOVA RIPIENE CON FORMAGGIO E SPINACI)

5 ounces frozen chopped spinach
12 hard boiled eggs
¼ cup grated Parmesan cheese
⅛ teaspoon ground nutmeg
½ cup milk
½ cup Ricotta cheese
Salt and pepper to taste

Cook spinach according to package directions, drain and squeeze out all liquid. Chop finely and set aside.

Cut eggs in half lengthwise, remove yolks and mash with a fork. Mix in the spinach, Parmesan cheese, nutmeg, milk, Ricotta cheese and salt and pepper to taste. Sprinkle egg whites with salt to taste and fill each with some of the mixture, mounding them well. Cover and chill until serving time.

Makes 24 appetizers

Tomatoes With Tuna and Yogurt
(POMODORI AL TONNO E YOGURT)

6 large, ripe, but firm tomatoes
8 ounces tuna fish in oil, drained and flaked
3 to 4 anchovy fillets, finely chopped
3 ounces, about ⅓ cup, yogurt
2 tablespoons parsley, finely chopped

Wipe tomatoes, slice off tops and reserve tops. With a spoon, scoop out seeds and discard. Scoop out juices and pulp and reserve.

In a food processor, process the pulp and juices, the tuna fish, anchovy fillets and yogurt to a puree. Stuff the mixture into the tomato shells, sprinkle with parsley and cover with reserved tops.

Serve cold.

Serves 6

Peas With Parma Ham

(PISELLI AL PROSCIUTTO)

1 small leek
4 tablespoons butter or margarine
1½ pounds fresh or frozen peas
½ cup hot chicken stock
Salt and pepper to taste
3 to 4 ounces Parma ham, cut into strips
Triangles of fried bread

Discard green part of leek and wash white part thoroughly. Cut crosswise into ¼ inch slices. Saute in the butter until leek is limp.

Add the peas and the stock and season with salt and pepper. Simmer for 10 to 15 minutes, until peas are tender. Toward end of cooking time, add ham and stir gently. Mixture should not be watery.

Serve on triangles of fried bread or on buttered toast triangles.

Serves 4

Smoked Tongue And Swiss Cheese Canapes

(CANAPES DI LINGUA AFFUMICATA E GROVIERA)

18 thin slices smoked or cured tongue
18 thin slices Swiss or Gruyere cheese
3 ounces mayonnaise
1 teaspoon mustard
18 (2-inch) toast rounds
Garnish of watercress

Shape tongue into 2-inch discs. Shape Swiss cheese into 1-inch discs.

Mix together mayonnaise and mustard. Spread toast rounds with some of the mixture. Layer each with a disc of tongue and one of Swiss cheese.

Serve on a platter with doilies and garnish with a tuft of watercress.

Serves 6

Stuffed Mushrooms

(FUNGHI FARCITI)

24 whole fresh mushrooms
2 tablespoons finely chopped onion
2 tablespoons butter or margarine
2 ounces (about 2 tablespoons) diced cooked ham
2 ounces (about 2 tablespoons) grated Parmesan cheese
1 tablespoon white flour
⅛ teaspoon salt
½ cup milk
Salt and pepper to taste
¼ cup fine, dry bread crumbs

Preheat oven to 350° F.

Remove stems from mushrooms. Chop stems. Cook stems and onion in 1 tablespoon of the butter until tender. Remove from heat. Stir in ham and Parmesan cheese. Set aside.

In a small saucepan, melt remaining butter. Stir in flour and salt, and mix until smooth. Add milk all at once. Cook and stir until thickened and bubbly. Add salt and pepper to taste. Remove from heat. Stir in ham mixture.

Fill each mushroom cap with some of the mixture. Sprinkle with bread crumbs. Place stuffed mushrooms in greased shallow baking dish. Bake in oven for 8 to 10 minutes or until mushrooms are tender.

Serves 6

Marinated Mushrooms
(FUNGHI MARINATI)

½ cup olive oil
2 tablespoons lemon juice
1 clove minced garlic
¾ teaspoon salt
½ teaspoon crushed dried oregano
¼ teaspoon black pepper
6 cups sliced fresh mushrooms
1 tablespoon bread crumbs
1 tablespoon chopped parsley

In a screw-top jar, combine oil, lemon juice, garlic, salt, oregano and pepper. Cover and shake well.

Pour over mushrooms, tossing gently to coat. Cover and let stand at room temperature about one hour, stirring occasionally.

To serve, drain mushrooms. Toss with bread crumbs and parsley.

Serves 6

Prosciutto And Fruits

(PROSCIUTTO CRUDO E FRUTTA)

Assorted fruits: cantaloupe, honeydew, figs, kiwi
½ pound thinly sliced prosciutto
Juice of one lemon
Leafy lettuce
2 limes or lemons, cut into wedges

Peel fruit and cut into bite size pieces. Sprinkle with lemon to prevent browning.

Cut prosciutto into 1-inch wide strips.

Using wooden picks, alternate fruit and prosciutto, threading each strip of prosciutto accordion style.

Serve with the lime or lemon wedges on a bed of leafy lettuce.

Serves 6

Fondue Piedmont

(FONDUE PIEMONTESE)

4 cups shredded Fontina or Gruyere cheese (about 1 pound)
2 tablespoons all-purpose flour
2 cups milk
2 egg yolks, slightly beaten
Bread sticks, or Italian bread, cubed

Coat cheese with the flour. In a 2-quart saucepan, heat milk over low heat. When warm, add cheese, stirring constantly until cheese is melted and mixture is smooth. Gradually stir about 1 cup of the hot mixture into the egg yolks, being careful not to curdle yolks. Stir this into remaining hot mixture. Cook and stir about 2 more minutes. Do not boil.

Transfer mixture to a fondue pot. Keep warm over fondue burner. Serve with breadsticks or bread cubes. Use fondue forks to spear and dip the bread cubes into the fondue pot.

Serves 4 to 6.

Grilled Mozzarella

(MOZZARELLA IN CARROZZA)

8 ounces Mozzarella, sliced
4 loaves Italian bread, crusts removed, and sliced ½-inch thick
3 eggs, well beaten
¼ cup milk
⅛ teaspoon dried thyme, crushed
¼ teaspoon salt
¾ cup fine, dry bread crumbs

Place Mozzarella cheese slices on half of the bread slices, trimming cheese to fit. Top with remaining bread slices.

Combine eggs, milk, thyme and salt. Dip both sides of sandwiches in egg mixture, then dip in bread crumbs. Press crumbs lightly so that they will adhere.

Saute on lightly greased griddle over medium-high heat about 8 minutes, or until crisp, turning once.

Serve warm. Makes 16 appetizers.

Serves 8

Florida Oysters

(OSTRICHE ALLA MANIERA DELLA FLORIDA)

6 dozen fresh oysters (72)
2 lemons
1 cup dry white wine
Pinch of pepper
3 teaspoons "A.1." sauce
Buttered rye bread crisps

Open fresh oysters, discarding those already open. Drain liquor and reserve in a container. Gently remove shells and dip oysters in their liquor. Reserve the larger valves of each oyster and clean them.

Drain the oyster liquor into a saucepan. Add lemon juice, white wine and pepper. Bring to boil, reduce heat, add oysters and simmer for 2 minutes. Remove from heat and allow oysters to cool in the stock. Remove oysters and arrange each on a reserved valve. Heat stock to boiling and reduce until it becomes of syrup consistency. Add "A.1" sauce and stir. Coat oysters with the sauce. Serve cold with a green garnish.

Serve with buttered rye bread toasts.

Serves 8

Crabmeat Baked In Pastry

(FAGOTTINI CON GRANCHI)

15 ounces frozen puff pastry
15 ounces crabmeat
6 tablespoons grated Parmesan cheese
3 tablespoons chopped parsley
3 cloves garlic, finely chopped
Salt and pepper to taste
1 egg, beaten, for sealing pastry

Divide pastry into six parts. Roll each piece out to a thickness of ¼ inch and cut into 8-inch squares. Mix the crabmeat, cheese, parsley, garlic and salt and pepper. Divide into six parts.

Preheat oven to 425 ° F.

Pile each of the six mounds of crabmeat mixture onto center of each square of pastry. Pull pastry up around the crabmeat to enclose and press together with fingers to pleat and seal. Make sure the pastry sticks well.

Grease an oven dish and place pouches on it. Brush each pouch with the beaten egg and bake for approximately 25 minutes or until golden. Serve immediately.

Serves 6

Potato-Cheese Croquettes
(CROCCHETTE DI PATATE AL FORMAGGIO)

1¼ pounds potatoes
2 tablespoons butter, softened
¼ cup grated Parmesan cheese
4 eggs
¼ teaspoon grated nutmeg
Salt and pepper to taste
2 cups frying oil
2½ cups fresh bread crumbs

Peel and boil potatoes until cooked through. Drain and mash them thoroughly. Add the butter, cheese, 2 of the eggs, nutmeg and salt and pepper to taste. Mix well. Take a portion of the mixture and roll into a sausage-shaped croquette. Repeat until all of the mixture is used.

Beat two remaining eggs lightly. Dip croquettes into the egg, then roll in bread crumbs.

Heat oil to 375° F. and deep fry the croquettes, several at a time, until golden. Drain on paper towels.

Serves 4

Asparagus Milanese
(ASPARAGI ALLA MILANESE)

3 pounds asparagus
4 quarts water
4½ ounces grated Parmesan or Swiss cheese
12 tablespoons butter
12 eggs
Salt to taste

With a vegetable peeler, scrape asparagus stems. Repeatedly wash in cold water to remove all traces of sand. Tie into six bundles with a thin thread. Cut tough, woody bottoms of asparagus to equalize length of bundles.

Heat water to boiling in a medium-size pot. Place asparagus bundles upright, with stems down, in boiling water and cook, simmering gently for 15 minutes. Do not overcook. Remove from water and drain well on paper toweling.

Arrange asparagus on six individual plates. Cut and remove threads. Sprinkle tips with grated cheese.

Melt 2 tablespoons of the butter in a skillet and allow to brown. Break two eggs into the butter, stir, salt to taste, and cook until soft curds form. Arrange shirred eggs evenly over asparagus on one plate, and pour on butter from skillet over all. Repeat process for all 6 portions.

Serves 6

Eggplant Caponata
(CAPONATA DI MELANZANE)

½ cup olive oil
½ cup celery
½ cup onions
2 pounds eggplant, peeled and cut into ½-inch cubes
1 (16-ounce) can peeled tomatoes, drained and cut up
2 tablespoons wine vinegar
1 teaspoon sugar
Salt and pepper to taste
1 tablespoon capers
½ cup sliced pitted ripe olives
2 tablespoons pine nuts
1 tablespoon snipped parsley

Heat oil in skillet to medium-high. Add celery and onion and cook for approximately 5 minutes or until onions are limp. Add eggplant cubes and saute just until tender. Add tomatoes, wine vinegar, sugar, salt and pepper. Cook over low heat for 5 minutes, stirring occasionally. Remove from heat.

Stir in capers, olives, pine nuts and parsley. Cover and chill until serving time.

Serves 6

Soups and Stews

Pasta in Broth

(PASTINA IN BRODO)

6 cups beef or chicken broth
1 cup small pasta, such as orzo*
4 tablespoons grated Parmesan cheese
1 tablespoon chopped fresh parsley

In a large pot, bring beef or chicken broth to a boil. Add pasta and simmer, uncovered, just until pasta is tender.

Ladle soup into bowls and sprinkle each serving with some of the cheese and the chopped parsley.

Serves 4 to 6

*Note: Orzo is a barley-shaped pasta made from wheat flour and is available in most Gourmet food shops.

Chicken Soup With Poached Eggs
(BRODO DI POLLO CON UOVA IN CAMICIA)

4 slices Italian bread, cut ½ inch thick
4 eggs
¼ cup butter or margarine
4 cups rich chicken broth
¼ cup grated Parmesan cheese

In a skillet melt butter or margarine. Add bread slices and saute for 4 to 5 minutes or until golden, turning once. Place toasted bread slice in each of 4 soup bowls.

To poach eggs, lightly grease a 10-inch skillet. Add about 1½ inches water to skillet and bring to a boil. Reduce heat to simmer. Carefully slide eggs, one at a time, into water, keeping eggs evenly spaced. Simmer, uncovered, for 3 to 5 minutes. Do not let water boil. When eggs are cooked to desired doneness, lift out with slotted spoon.

Place an egg on toasted bread slice in each bowl. Heat broth to a simmer and carefully pour into bowls around the eggs. Sprinkle with Parmesan cheese.

Serves 4

Stracciatella

(STRACCIATELLA)

3½ cups chicken broth
½ cup water
¼ cup tripolini or other small pasta
2 tablespoons grated Parmesan cheese
1 tablespoon snipped parsley
Dash freshly ground nutmeg
1 well beaten egg

In a saucepan bring broth and water to a boil. Add tripolini and simmer, just until pasta is tender. Reduce heat. Stir in Parmesan, parsley and nutmeg. Slowly pour egg into simmering broth. Stir once gently. Serve immediately, with more cheese if desired.

Serves 4

Minestrone Genoa Style
(MINESTRONE ALLA GENOVESE)

MINESTRONE:
½ pound dried white beans
2 quarts water
½ pound medium large cabbage
2 medium large potatoes
2 stalks celery
½ pound rice or 12 ounces small macaroni
½ pound small zucchini
1 cup peas, shelled or frozen and thawed
½ pound broad beans
½ pound green string beans

PESTO:
2 ounces fresh basil leaves
3 ounces Romano cheese
2 cloves garlic
8 ounces olive oil
Pinch of pepper
Salt to taste

Wash dried beans well and soak in water overnight. Place them in a large pot with the water and bring to a boil. Reduce heat and simmer until beans are cooked. Finely chop all vegetables and drop into simmering water. Continue to cook for half an hour at a simmer. Add rice or small macaroni and cook for 15 to 20 minutes longer.

To prepare Pesto, combine basil, grated cheese, a pinch of salt and garlic. Place in a mortar and pound with pestle until finely shredded. Blend in oil and a scant cup of the soup and mix well. Add to minestrone, stirring well. You may use a food processor instead of mortar. As a variation, use any kind of vegetables in season.

Serves 6

Lobster Soup

(MINESTRA D'ARAGOSTA)

½ cup olive oil
1 medium large onion, chopped
2 stalks celery, sliced crosswise
2 cloves garlic
1 (4-pound) lobster
1 cup dry white wine
½ pound ripe fresh tomatoes, peeled, seeded and chopped
3 quarts water
Salt to taste
1 teaspoon white pepper
12 ounces small pasta, cooked
1 sprig fresh tarragon, finely chopped

Heat oil in a saucepan and saute onions, celery and whole garlic cloves until limp.

Cut lobster head lengthwise and the tail crosswise. Arrange in a large saucepan. Saute for a few minutes, then add wine. Continue sauteing until wine evaporates completely. Add the chopped tomatoes and salt. Cover and cook for 5 minutes, then add water. Cover and cook about 20 more minutes or until lobster is cooked.

Remove lobster meat from shell and dice. Strain the stock through cheesecloth and reduce to half over high heat. Return lobster meat to strained stock. Reheat to boiling. Add pasta, lower heat and simmer a few more minutes. Add salt and pepper to taste and the chopped tarragon leaves. Serve hot.

Serves 6

Chicken And Rice Soup "Bella Romagna"

(MINESTRA DI POLLO E RISO "BELLA ROMAGNA")

3 ounces salt pork, cut into cubes
6 ounces leeks (white part only) cleaned thoroughly and sliced
3 ounces butter (about ⅔ stick)
1½ pounds boneless chicken, coarsley chopped
3 quarts water
½ pound cabbage, shredded
10 ounces rice (1¼ cups)
Salt to taste
1 teaspoon white pepper

Combine cubed salt pork, sliced leeks and half the butter in a saucepan. Saute for 5 minutes. Add chicken and let brown lightly for 5 minutes. Add water and salt. Heat to boiling, then reduce heat and simmer for 20 minutes.

Add cabbage and rice and continue cooking for about 20 minutes more or until rice is done. Add salt and pepper and remaining butter cut into pieces.

Serves 6

Fish Stew

(RAGU DI PESCE)

2½ pounds fish fillets (grouper, snapper, tuna)
Salt and pepper to taste
Flour for dusting
1¼ cups olive oil
2 cloves garlic, crushed
½ cup dry white wine
2 small onions, sliced
1½ pounds ripe tomatoes, peeled, seeded and pureed
1 cup hot water

Dry fish on paper toweling and cut into fairly thick slices. Sprinkle with salt and pepper and dust with flour.

Heat the oil in a large saute pan and when hot, add one clove of mashed garlic. Saute lightly, then add the fish fillets. Saute until lightly brown on both sides, turning carefully with a spatula. Add the wine and cook until wine evaporates. Discard the garlic, and remove fish from pan. Keep hot.

Add remaining crushed garlic and onion to the pan and saute until onion is limp. Return fish to pan and cook for a few minutes more, then add tomatoes and cook for another 5 minutes. Add salt and pepper if required, then add a cup of hot water and cook for 15 to 20 minutes. Serve at once.

Serves 4

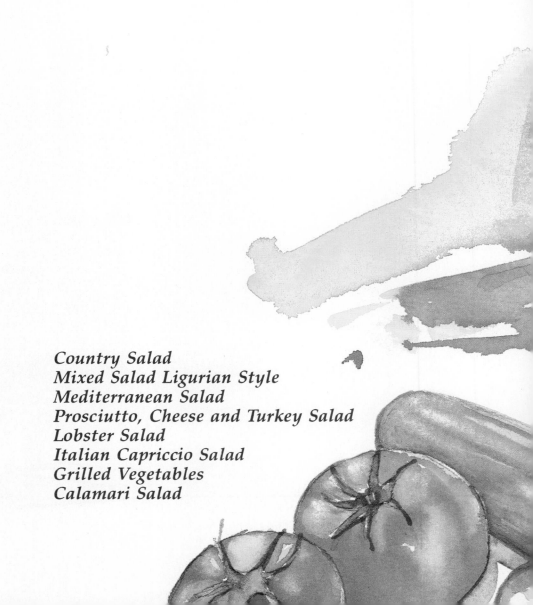

Country Salad
Mixed Salad Ligurian Style
Mediterranean Salad
Prosciutto, Cheese and Turkey Salad
Lobster Salad
Italian Capriccio Salad
Grilled Vegetables
Calamari Salad

Salads and Vegetables

Country Salad

(INSALATA PAESANA)

2 pounds potatoes
1 head escarole
1 head red leaf lettuce
2 white onions, peeled and thinly sliced
1 cup smoked ham, cut into 1 inch strips
½ cup smoked bacon, cut into 1 inch strips and sauteed
½ cup olive oil
Juice from one lemon
1 to 2 tablespoons white wine vinegar, to taste
1 teaspoon Coleman's powdered mustard
Ground green pepper and salt to taste

Boil potatoes until cooked through. Cool and peel. Cut into thin slices. Place in cold water to sweeten.

Wash salad greens and dry on paper towels. Tear them into edible pieces and place in a large salad bowl. Add the potatoes, (drain and dried) onion rings, smoked ham and bacon.

Mix together olive oil, lemon juice, vinegar, mustard and salt and pepper. Pour over salad greens and toss gently to blend. Serve at once.

Serves 6

Mixed Salad Ligurian Style

(INSALATA ALLA LIGURE)

3 cloves garlic, peeled and partially mashed
6 large salad tomatoes, cut into wedges
1 large sweet pepper, cored, seeded and cut into strips
1 cucumber, peeled and thinly sliced
10 basil leaves, coarsely chopped
2 large anchovy fillets, finely chopped
2 teaspoons oregano
12 black olives, pitted
2 hard boiled eggs, quartered
1 small can tuna fish in oil, flaked
3 tablespoons extra virgin olive oil
Salt and pepper to taste

Rub a large salad bowl with the garlic. Discard garlic. Add all remaining ingredients in the order given, adding olive oil last with salt and pepper. Mix gently until oil coats all ingredients. Marinate for one hour, then stir again gently, and serve on chilled salad plates.

Serves 6

Mediterranean Salad

(INSALATA MEDITERRANEA)

6 firm, ripe tomatoes
1 head Boston lettuce
1 head endive or chicory
24 salted fillets of anchovy in oil
40 small black olives
4 lemons cut in slices
½ cup olive oil
1 tablespoon freshly ground pepper
1 tablespoon red wine vinegar
Salt to taste

Slice tomatoes and set aside. Cut lettuce into edible pieces.

Divide tomatoes and lettuce among six plates. Top each with 3 to 4 anchovy fillets and 5 or 6 black olives. Arrange slices of lemon around on each plate.

Mix the olive oil, vinegar, ground pepper and salt and pour ingredients on each plate.

Serves 6

Prosciutto, Cheese and Turkey Salad

(INSALATA DI PROSCIUTTO, FORMAGGIO E TACCHINO)

4 ripe tomatoes
2 small heads lettuce (use different kinds)
½ clove garlic, slightly mashed
2 cups cooked turkey, cut into thin strips
1 cup Swiss cheese, cut into thin strips
8 ounces prosciutto, cut into thin strips
½ cup olive oil
2 tablespoons lemon juice
Salt and pepper to taste
2 tablespoons Italian parsley, chopped

Cut tomatoes into wedges. tear lettuce into bite-size pieces. Rub the inside of a wooden bowl with the clove of garlic, and add turkey, cheese and ham.

In a small bowl, mix olive oil, lemon juice and salt and pepper. Pour over salad greens and toss lightly, but well. Garnish with parsley.

Serves 6

Lobster Salad

(INSALATA DI ARAGOSTA)

2 pounds poached lobster meat, sliced
1 pound carrots, cooked and cut into small cubes
½ pound, fresh or frozen peas, cooked
1 pound potatoes (preferrably yellow waxy ones), cooked and cut
into small cubes
1 cup mayonnaise
Salt and black pepper to taste
2 hard boiled eggs

Place lobster, carrots, peas and potatoes in a bowl. Add mayonnaise and salt and pepper. Mix all ingredients carefully. Arrange on a flat, oval dish and decorate with slices of hard-boiled eggs.

You may arrange the lobster slices on top of the mixed vegetables, if desired.

Serves 6 to 8

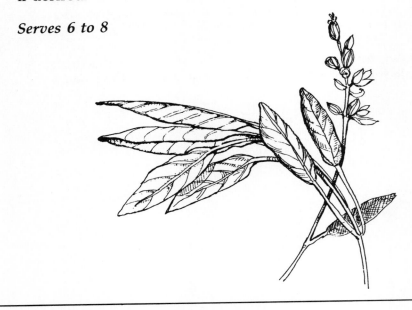

Italian Capriccio Salad

(INSALATA CAPRICCIOSA)

4 ounces prosciutto
4 ounces Fontina cheese
1 carrot
1 stalk white celery
2 small sweet pickles
½ cup cooked green peas
½ cup Mayonnaise
½ tablespoon Worcestershire sauce
Salt and black pepper to taste
2 hard-boiled eggs

Cut prosciutto and Fontina cheese into fine julienne strips. Clean carrot, discard strings from celery and wash well. Drain on paper towels. Cut carrot, celery and pickles into julienne strips and mix with ham and cheese. Mix in peas.

Add mayonnaise, Worcestershire sauce and salt and pepper to mixture and toss well.

Cut hard-boiled eggs into slices and use to garnish the salad.

Serves 6

Grilled Vegetables
(VERDURE GRIGLIATE ALLA "COSTA")

4 small zucchini, sliced
4 bell-peppers cut in slices
1 eggplant, sliced crosswise ¼-inch thick
4 tomatoes, sliced
2 Idaho potatoes, sliced ⅛-inch thick
4 tablespoons extra virgin olive oil
1 bunch basil leaves
1 pinch dried oregano
Salt, pepper and minced garlic to taste.

Grill the vegetables, without seasoning, on each side for about 2 to 3 minutes. Place on serving tray.

Mix with oil, herbs, salt, pepper and minced garlic. Pour over grilled vegetables.

Serves 4

Calamari Salad

(INSALATA DI CALAMARI)

3 pounds fresh calamari (or frozen, thawed)
¼ cup olive oil
Juice of one lemon
6 scallions with tops
1 red bell pepper, cored and seeded
2 tablespoons fresh chopped basil, sliced into ribbons
2 tablespoons chopped parsley
1 can drained, pitted Manzanilla olives

Clean, wash and dry calamari with paper toweling. Slice into rings. Cut tentacle clusters in two. Place rings and tentacles in boiling, lightly salted water, lower heat and simmer for approximately 20 minutes. Drain throughly.

Mix oil and lemon juice and add the drained calamari, tossing well. Chill.

Reserve several inches of green scallion tops. Thinly slice remaining white bulbs and add to the calamari.

Cut scallion tops and red pepper into very thin strips, seal in plastic wrap and refrigerate until serving time.

When ready to serve, add scallion tops, red pepper strips, basil, parsley and pitted olives to calamari.

Gently mix and serve chilled.

Serves 6

Focaccia, Genoa Style
  With Sage
  With Rosemary
  With Black Olives
  With Onion
Olive-Pepper Bread
Whole Wheat Homestyle Bread
Perfect White Bread
White Flour Rolls

Breads

Focaccia, Genoa Style
(FOCACCIA ALLA GENOVESE)

2 ounces fresh or dried yeast
Pinch of salt
8 cups all-purpose flour
10 tablespoons olive oil

Dissolve yeast in a cup of lukewarm water with salt. Let stand 5 minutes to activate yeast.

Sift flour into a large bowl and make a well in the center. Add the yeast mixture and gradually bring in the flour from the sides of the bowl. Mix well, cover bowl and keep in a warm place for 20 minutes.

Knead the dough and add more liquid if needed to make a firm dough. The dough should be firm enough to come away from the sides of the bowl. Cover dough with a wet towel and keep it in a warm place until it doubles in size, approximately one hour. Punch dough down and knead in six tablespoons of the olive oil. Divide the dough into workable quantities and roll out each to a thickness of ½ inch. Preheat oven to 400° F.

Place the dough on a baking dish that has been oiled with some of the remaining 4 tablespoons olive oil. Prick the dough all over with a fork, then dribble with remaining olive oil. Sprinkle with salt and bake in oven for approximately 20 minutes, or until top is golden.

Focaccia is usually cut into slices 1½ inches wide and 2 to 3 inches long. It can be eaten by itself or during the meal.

Serves 6 to 8

Focaccia With Sage
(FOCACCIA ALLA SALVIA)

Use the same ingredients and techniques as those used in recipe for Focaccia, Genoa Style, but add 20 sage leaves, finely chopped, to the dough with the oil.

Focaccia With Rosemary
(FOCACCIA AL ROSMARINO)

Use the same ingredients and techniques as those used in recipe for Focaccia, Genoa Style, but add 4 tablespoons fresh rosemary leaves to the dough with the oil.

Focaccia With Black Olives
(FOCACCIA CON OLIVE)

Use the same ingredients and techniques as those used in recipe for Focaccia, Genoa Style, but add 6 ounces of finely chopped black olives to the dough with the oil.

Focaccia With Onion
(FOCACCIA CON CIPOLLE)

Use the same ingredients and techniques as those used in recipe for Focaccia, Genoa Style, but spread top with 1 cup sliced onion mixed with 2 tablespoons olive oil.

Olive-Pepper Bread

(PANE CON OLIVE E PEPERONI)

For the Bread:
1 envelope dried yeast
1 tablespoon sugar
½ cup lukewarm water
3 cups flour, or more, as needed
Salt to taste
2 tablespoons olive oil

For the filling:
2 tablespoons olive oil
½ medium onion, chopped
1 red bell pepper, seeded and chopped
1 green bell pepper, seeded and chopped
½ cup black olives, chopped
½ cup green olives, chopped
Salt and black pepper to taste

Place the dried yeast and the sugar in the warm water, mix well and let stand until it foams. Place the flour and salt in a food processor and gradually add the yeast-water and the olive oil. Add more water and/or more flour, if needed. Process mixture until it forms a fairly firm ball.

Remove from processor and knead for a few minutes, until dough is smooth. Form into a ball and place in a greased pan. Cover with plastic wrap, place in a warm spot and let rise until double in bulk.

While dough is rising, place oil for filling in a saute pan and when it is medium-hot, add onion and the red and green bell peppers. Saute until the peppers are cooked. Add the olives and season to taste.

continued

Heat oven to 400° F.

When the bread dough has doubled in bulk, punch it down and roll it into a rectangle. Spread the surface with the pepper-olive mixture. Roll as tightly as possible into a long loaf, the shape of French bread. Place in a greased French bread pan and let rise until double in bulk. Place in 400° F. oven and bake for ten minutes. Reduce heat to 350° F. and bake for approximately 30 minutes longer or until loaf is golden.

Cool to warm or room temperature and slice to serve.

Makes 1 large loaf

Whole Wheat Homestyle Bread

(PANE CASALINGO AL FRUMENTO)

¾ cup milk
3 teaspoons sugar
2 teaspoons salt
2 ounces butter or margarine
¼ cup molasses
1 cup warm water
2 envelopes dry yeast
4 cups whole wheat flour
2 cups all purpose flour

Grease 2 loaf pans and set aside.

Place milk in a saucepan over low heat and add sugar, salt, butter and molasses. Mix until sugar is dissolved and butter is melted. Cool to lukewarm.

Measure warm water into a large, warm bowl and mix in the yeast. When it is dissolved, add the lukewarm milk mixture and half the flours. Beat until smooth. Add enough of the remaining flours (more if necessary) to make a soft dough and knead until smooth and elastic.

Cover dough and let rise until doubled in bulk, about 1 hour.

Punch dough down and place on a lightly floured work surface. Divide in half and shape into loaves. Place in greased pans. Cover and let rise in warm place until doubled in bulk.

While loaves are rising, preheat over to 400° F.

Bake loaves 25 to 30 minutes. Remove from pans and cool on racks.

Makes **2**

Perfect White Bread
(PANE BIANCO)

2 cups warm water
2 envelopes dry yeast
2 teaspoons salt
1 tablespoon melted butter or margarine
6 cups all purpose flour
¼ cup corn meal
1 egg white
1 tablespoon cold water

Lightly grease 2 baking sheets and set aside. Measure 1 tablespoon of the warm water into a warm bowl and add the yeast. When yeast is dissolved, add salt, butter and flour and knead until well blended. Add as much of second cup of warm water as needed to make a firm but pliable dough.

Place dough in a greased bowl, cover and let rise in a warm place until doubled in bulk, about 1 hour. Punch dough down and place on a lightly floured work surface. Divide into 2 parts. Roll each portion into a rectangle. Beginning at long side, roll up dough tightly toward you. Seal edges by pinching them together.

Lightly sprinkle greased baking sheets with cornmeal. Place loaves on the baking sheets, cover and let rise in a warm place until doubled in bulk.

While loaves are rising, preheat oven to 450° F. Using a sharp knife, carefully make 4 diagonal cuts on each loaf. Bake in oven for 25 minutes. Meanwhile, in a small bowl, combine egg white and cold water. Brush top and sides of each loaf with mixture and bake 5 minutes longer. Remove from sheets and cool on racks.

Makes 2

White Flour Rolls

(PANINI BIANCHI)

2 pounds all-purpose flour
1½ ounces fresh or dried yeast
1 tablespoon sugar
2 cups lukewarm water
1 teaspoon salt
1 tablespoon malt
2 tablespoons shortening (margarine, Crisco or lard), melted
  and cooled

Sift flour into a heap on a wooden work surface and make a well in the center. Dissolve yeast and sugar in lukewarm water. Pour the yeast mixture into center of the well, adding salt, malt and shortening. Mix well with hand, then bring the flour to the center, little by little, until all is incorporated. Knead for about 10 minutes, using more flour as needed to make an elastic dough.

Form dough into a round, cover and let rise for about 2 hours. Punch down and cut into small rounds. Place on a greased baking pan. Let rise ½ hour or until doubled. Bake in a 375° F. oven for 30 to 40 minutes. Reduce heat to 350° F. after 15 minutes of baking. Serve warm.

Soya Bread
(PANINI DI SOIA)

Make bread as per recipe above, adding 3 tablespoons soya sauce to the well with the yeast.

Butter Rolls
(PANINI AL BURRO)

Replace other shortening in recipe above with ¼ cup butter.

Serves 8

Spaghetti With Fresh Tomato And Basil Sauce
Spaghetti With Garlic And Red Pepper
Spaghetti Carbonara
Spaghetti With Sea Urchin Sauce
Green Lasagna Au Gratin
Baked Tagliatelle With Prosciutto And Artichokes
Fettuccine Alfredo
Stuffed Homemade Pasta With Basil Leave Sauce
Potato Gnocchi
Macaroni Alberto
Baked Macaroni Sicilian Style

Risotto Primavera
Sea Mountain Risotto
Champagne Risotto
Four-Cheese Risotto
Risotto Alla Milanese

Cheese And Rice Omelette, Italian Style
Lightly Fried Eggs With Fontina Cheese

Classic Polenta
Four-Cheese Polenta Timbale
Polenta With Mushroom Sauce

Pasta, Rice and Grains

Spaghetti With Fresh Tomato And Basil Sauce
(SPAGHETTI AL POMODORO E BASILICO)

2½ pounds fresh ripe tomatoes
⅓ cup Italian olive oil
½ cup chopped onion
3 cloves garlic
2 tablespoons chopped fresh basil
Salt and pepper to taste
1¼ pounds spaghetti
¾ cup Parmesan cheese
20 basil leaves

Wash, peel and chop tomatoes, discarding seeds. Heat oil in a moderately deep pan, add onion and garlic and saute until onion is limp. Discard garlic and add tomatoes, chopped basil and salt and pepper. Simmer for about 20 minutes over moderate heat.

While sauce is simmering, bring a large pot of water to boil. Add salt to taste and add spaghetti. Boil until spaghetti is "al dente," approximately 8 to 10 minutes. Drain spaghetti, toss with the sauce and the grated cheese.

Garnish each plate with some of the basil leaves. Serve at once.

Serves 8

Spaghetti With Garlic And Red Pepper

(SPAGHETTI ALL' AGLIO E PEPERONCINO PICCANTE)

2 tablespoons olive oil
4-6 large, ripe tomatoes, peeled and chopped
3 cloves garlic, finely chopped
1 teaspoon crushed red pepper
1 tablespoon chopped parsley
Salt to taste
1 pound spaghetti
½ cup freshly grated Parmesan cheese

Heat olive oil in a large skillet and add tomatoes, garlic and crushed pepper. Let simmer over low heat for 15 minutes. Add parsley and salt and simmer 2 minutes longer.

Meanwhile, heat 4 to 6 quarts water in a large pot. Add salt to taste and the spaghetti. Bring to boil and boil about 8 minutes, until spaghetti is "al dente." Do not over cook. Drain and add to the skillet. Heat through and serve sprinkled generously with Parmesan cheese.

Serves 4

Spaghetti Carbonara
(SPAGHETTI CARBONARA)

2 pounds spaghetti
1 teaspoon salt
¼ pound pancetta or bacon
1 cup heavy cream
4 egg yolks
½ cup grated Parmesan cheese
Salt and black pepper to taste

Place 3 to 4 quarts of water in a large pot and bring to boil. Break spaghetti strings in half and add to pot with 1 teaspoon salt. Drain.

Meanwhile cut pancetta or bacon into strips and saute in a large saute pan until most of fat is rendered. Remove from pan. Add drained spaghetti, cream and egg yolks. Mix quickly and well and saute over low heat for 1 or 2 minutes. Do not let eggs curdle. Add salt and black pepper to taste. Add Parmesan cheese and mix well. Serve immediately.

Serves 4 to 6

Spaghetti With Sea Urchin Sauce
(SPAGHETTI AI RICCI DI MARE)

4 tablespoons olive oil
2 cloves garlic, crushed
Eggs from six sea urchins
2 red sweet peppers, cut into strips
1 cup dry white wine
Salt and pepper to taste
¾ pound spaghetti

Heat oil in a large saute pan. Add garlic and when it is lightly golden, add the sea urchin eggs. Stir and cook over low heat for about 10 minutes. Add red pepper strips and saute for approximately 5 more minutes. Make certain not to scorch peppers. Add wine and continue sauteing over low heat for another 35 minutes, or a total of 50 minutes. If the sauce becomes too dry, add more wine. Salt and pepper to taste.

Fill a large pot with 4 to 6 quarts water. Bring to boil, add salt and spaghetti. Cook "al dente" and drain. Place in a spaghetti platter and top with sea urchin sauce. Serve hot.

NOTE: We owe this recipe to an exceptional chef, Captain Mario Garbarino Master of MTS DAPHNE who created and tested it onboard ship.

Serves 4

Green Lasagna Au Gratin

(LASAGNE VERDI AL GRATIN)

LASAGNE:

2 pounds flour
½ cup pureed spinach
4 eggs
Salt to taste

Combine flour, spinach puree, salt and eggs. Knead well into a smooth dough and let stand ½ hour covered. Roll out on board into thin round or rectangle. Cut into 3-inch squares.

CREAM SAUCE:

6 tablespoons butter
6 tablespoons flour
2 cups milk, heated to boiling
⅔ to 1 cup grated Parmesan cheese
4 cups (1 pound) meat sauce, recipe below
Pinch of nutmeg

Melt butter in a sauce pan and add flour. Stir until smooth and flour becomes yellowish. Pour hot milk into mixture and whisk vigorously until sauce is well blended and smooth. Add salt to taste and nutmeg and simmer for about 20 minutes over low heat, stirring constantly.

continued

MEAT SAUCE:

2 tablespoons olive oil
½ medium onion, chopped
1 clove garlic, chopped
1 pound lean ground beef
4 large, ripe tomatoes, peeled, seeded and chopped

Heat olive oil in large sauce pan. Add onion and garlic and saute until onion is limp. Add ground beef and saute until lightly browned. Add tomatoes, mix in well and simmer over medium-low heat for approximately 15 minutes.

To assemble, preheat oven to 350° F. Bring a large pot containing 4 quarts water to a boil. Add salt to taste. Add lasagna squares and simmer for no more than 5 minutes, until squares are "al dente." Drain and sprinkle with fresh water to cool, then spread on a napkin.

Butter one or more deep baking pans and spread a little cream sauce on bottom. Arrange first layer of lasagna. Spread a layer of meat sauce, then sprinkle with grated cheese. Continue to layer, placing lasagna noddles on top. Spread remaining cream sauce and sprinkle with cheese. Dot with butter if desired and bake in preheated oven for 20 minutes or until heated through.

Serves 6

Baked Tagliatelle With Prosciutto And Artichokes

(TAGLIATELLE AL FORNO CON PROSCIUTTO E CARCIOFI)

6 fresh small artichokes
Juice of ½ lemon
2 tablespoons olive oil
1 medium onion, finely chopped
4 ounces prosciutto, cut into ¼ inch strips
5 tablespoons dry white wine
3 large ripe tomatoes, peeled, seeded and chopped
4 tablespoons chopped parsley
Salt and pepper to taste
1½ pounds fresh made, or 20 ounces dried tagliatelle
½ cup grated Parmesan cheese
1 cup heavy cream

Clean and trim artichokes, retaining only the bottoms. Cut into slices and place in a bowl with water and the lemon juice. Heat olive oil in a saucepan, add onion and saute until limp. Add prosciutto and drained artichokes and saute for 3 minutes, turning frequently. Add wine and when evaporated, add tomatoes. Simmer over medium-low heat until artichokes are tender (10 to 15 minutes). Add parsley and salt and pepper to taste.

Meanwhile, heat 4 to 6 quarts of water in a large pot. When water comes to a boil, add salt to taste and add the tagliatelle. Preheat oven to 400° F. When cooked "al dente," drain pasta and mix with sauce, half the Parmesan cheese and heavy cream. Butter a baking dish large enough to hold the mixture. Place in baking dish, sprinkle with remaining cheese and bake for approximately 10 minutes. Serve hot.

Serves 6

Fettuccine Alfredo
(FETTUCCINE ALFREDO)

1 pound wide noodles (such as fettuccine)
1 cup cooked ham strips
4 egg yolks
2 cups heavy cream
½ cup butter
1 cup freshly grated Parmesan cheese
Salt and black pepper to taste

In a large pot, heat 4 quarts water until boiling. Add salt to taste and the noodles. Boil until just tender (about 5 minutes). Drain and keep warm.

Meanwhile blend egg yolks and cream together. Set aside. Place butter in a large saute pan and melt. Add ham and saute lightly for several minutes. Add noodles and heat through. Add egg yolks mixed with cream and gently fold in until all the cream mixture is well blended. Add grated cheese and serve immediately.

Serves 4

Stuffed Homemade Pasta With Pesto

(CAPPELLACCI AL PESTO)

PASTA:
4 cups flour
4 eggs
½ cup water
Pinch of salt

Sift flour and salt onto board and make well in center of flour. Combine eggs with water and beat lightly. Pour egg mixture slowly into well, bringing the dough slowly into the well and combining until dough forms a firm ball. Cut dough in half and roll each into a ball. Let rest for 10 minutes under a bowl. Roll each ball of dough out on lightly floured board as thinly as possible.

Place 1 scant tablespoon of the stuffing (instructions below) at intervals along edge of dough and in rows. Cover with another sheet of dough, and cut them out with a pastry-wheel, in squares or rounds, as for ravioli or agnolotti. Make sure edges are sealed.

Place 4 quarts water in a large pot and bring to boil. Salt to taste and add the cappellacci carefully. Simmer lightly until they come to top and are sufficiently cooked. Drain and place on a bowl-shaped platter.

continued

STUFFING:

2 cups cleaned spinach leaves
1 onion
1 stalk celery
2 cloves garlic
Pinch of marjoram
1 tablespoon chopped parsley
2 tablespoons olive oil
1 cup Ricotta
2 eggs
2 tablespoons grated Parmesan cheese
Nutmeg, salt and pepper to taste

Cook, drain and squeeze all liquid from spinach.

Chop or lightly process in food processor with all other ingredients except Ricotta, eggs and Parmesan cheese. Saute in 2 tablespoons olive oil for several minutes. Cool and add Ricotta, cheese, eggs and seasonings and mix well.

PESTO:

4 bunches of basil (about 2 cups)
¼ cup pine nuts
2 cloves garlic
3-4 tablespoons olive oil
⅔ to 1 cup Parmesan cheese

Place basil leaves, pine nuts, garlic and salt into food processor. Process until mixture is finely chopped and smooth. While processor is on, slowly add olive oil in a thin stream. Add Parmesan cheese and process until well combined.

To assemble, top pasta with pesto and sprinkle with grated cheese.

Serves 4 to 6

Potato Gnocchi
(GNOCCHI DI PATATE)

1¼ pounds potatoes
Salt to taste
1 cup flour, or more as needed
½ cup grated Parmesan cheese
¼ pound Fontina cheese, thinly sliced
½ cup cream

Cook potatoes in their skins in salted water until tender. Remove skin and mash. Allow to cool slightly before adding flour. Mix in flour and knead lightly to form a soft dough. Slice off a portion and roll into a long rope, about 1-inch in diameter. Cut rope into approximately 1¼ inch lengths (smaller or larger if desired). Roll each length over the prongs of a fork, pressing lightly with the thumb to obtain a ridged effect. Repeat until all dough is used. Preheat oven to 400° F. Cook the gnocchi in boiling water, and remove with a slotted spoon when they rise to the surface. Transfer gnocchi to a buttered, ovenproof dish, and sprinkle with Parmesan cheese. Arrange the cheese on top. Pour cream over top and place in preheated oven for about 10 minutes or until top is golden.

Variations:

Spinach Gnocchi
(GNOCCHI VERDI)
Use recipe above, but add 4 ounces of cooked, pureed spinach to the potatoes and flour when preparing gnocchi.

Pink Gnocchi
(GNOCCHI ROSA)
Add about 2 ounces of tomato paste to the potatoes and flour when preparing gnocchi.

Serves 6

Macaroni Alberto
(MACCHERONI ALBERTO)

2 tablespoons butter
⅓ cup olive oil
1 small clove garlic, minced
½ large onion, minced
¼ cup parsley, minced
⅓ teaspoon curry powder
2 pounds fresh peeled and chopped tomatoes
Salt and pepper to taste
½ cup cream cheese
1 pound macaroni

Melt butter and oil in a large saucepan. Add garlic and onion and saute until onions are limp. Add parsley, curry and tomatoes and simmer for 15 to 20 minutes. Add salt and pepper to taste. Add cream cheese and mix in well. Simmer a minute longer.

While sauce is simmering, place a large pot of water to boil. When water is boiling, add salt to taste and the macaroni. When macaroni is "al dente," drain and place in a warm bowl or cupped platter. Pour sauce over macaroni and serve.

Note: you may, if you wish, add parmesan cheese, but the recipe does not call for it.

Serves 4 to 6

Baked Macaroni Sicilian Style

(MACCHERONI ALLA SICILIANA)

5 small eggplants
1 cup olive oil
1 clove garlic, chopped
½ large onion, chopped
2½ pounds fresh, peeled and chopped tomatoes
1 teaspoon dried oregano
Salt and black pepper to taste
½ pound diced Mozzarella cheese
¼ pound finely diced Parmesan cheese
10 basil leaves
1 pound macaroni

Heat oven to 350° F.

Dice two eggplants, fry ¼ cup of oil, and set aside. Slice three remaining eggplants lengthwise, and fry, using as much oil as necessary. Set aside.

Make tomato sauce by placing the remaining olive oil (no more than 2 tablespoons) in a large saucepan. Add garlic and onion and saute until limp. Add the chopped tomatoes and oregano and simmer 15 to 20 minutes. Salt and pepper to taste.

Fill a large pot with water and bring to a boil. Add salt and macaroni and boil until "al dente." Drain.

Mix together macaroni, diced eggplant, tomato sauce, Mozzarella and Parmesan cheese. Place in an oven-resistant casserole and lay slices of eggplant on top. Bake in heated oven for 15 to 20 minutes or until heated through and bubbly. Serve hot.

Serves 4 to 5

Risotto Primavera

(RISOTTO PRIMAVERA)

3 tablespoons butter
1 onion, finely chopped
1 sweet red pepper, seeded and sliced lengthwise
½ cup fresh mushrooms, quartered
½ cup fresh or frozen peas
1 small eggplant, diced
½ cup celery, thinly sliced
1 medium carrot, shredded
1 pound Arborio rice
½ cup dry white wine
4 to 6 cups hot chicken broth
⅓ cup grated Parmesan cheese
Salt and black pepper to taste

In a 3-quart saucepan heat butter and add onion and pepper. Saute until onion is limp. Add remaining vegetables, and when they are beginning to soften, add rice. Mix well and add the wine. Reduce heat and when wine has evaporated, add 2 cups of chicken broth. Stir continually until broth has evaporated. Add 2 more cups broth and continue to stir (adding more broth as needed) until rice is cooked, about 20 minutes. Add Parmesan cheese and salt and pepper. Serve immediately.

Serve 6 to 8

Sea Mountain Risotto

(RISOTTO MAREMONTI)

4 tablespoons butter
½ cup chopped leeks (white part only)
2 slices bacon, finely sliced
½ pound mushrooms, quartered
5 ounces frozen peas
1 pound Arborio rice
1 7½ ounce can minced clams, drained, liquid reserved
⅓ pound peeled small shrimp
½ cup dry white wine
6 cups hot beef broth
2 tablespoons chopped parsley
Salt and pepper to taste.

Heat 2 tablespoons of butter in a saucepan. Add leeks and bacon and saute until leeks are limp. Add mushrooms and peas and saute a few minutes more. Add rice and mix in well. Add clams and shrimp and saute 1 more minute. Add wine and cook until wine is evaporated. Add reserved clam juice and 1 cup of broth. Reduce heat and stir mixture continually until broth has evaporated. Continue to add broth and stir until each addition has evaporated and rice is cooked, about 20 minutes. Add remaining butter, parsley and salt and pepper to taste. Serve immediately.

Serves 6

Champagne Risotto
(RISOTTO ALLO CHAMPAGNE)

2 tablespoons cooking oil
4 tablespoons butter
1 onion, quartered
1 pound Arborio* rice
½ bottle dry champagne
4 cups hot veal or chicken broth
Salt and black pepper to taste

Heat oil and 2 tablespoons of butter in a 3 quart saucepan. Add onion and saute until golden. Discard onion. Add the rice and stir well for two minutes. Add 1 cup of champagne, increase heat and when it has evaporated, reduce heat to medium-low and add 2 cups of broth. Stir continually until broth has evaporated. Add as much of remaining broth as necessary and continue stirring until rice is nearly cooked. When final addition of broth has evaporated, add remaining champagne and continue to cook and stir until champagne has evaporated and rice is cooked. Rice should have a creamy consistency when cooking is completed. Add remaining butter and salt and pepper to taste. Serve hot.

*NOTE: A special Italian-style rice available in most Gourmet food shops.

Serves 6

Four-Cheese Risotto

(RISOTTO AI QUATTRO FORMAGGI)

½ cup (1 stick) butter
1 medium onion, finely diced
1 pound Arborio rice
6 cups consomme
½ cup diced Bel Paese cheese
½ cup diced Fontina cheese
½ cup diced Mozzarella cheese
½ cup Parmesan cheese
Salt to taste

In a casserole or large saucepan melt 4 tablespoon of the butter, add onion and saute until limp. Add rice and stir until butter has been absorbed. Gradually add the consomme and stir continuously for about 15 minutes, until consomme has been absorbed. Add the cheeses, one at a time, adding the Mozzarella last. Stir continuously. When well mixed add remaining butter and the grated Parmesan cheese. Salt to taste and serve.

Serves 6

Risotto Alla Milanese

(RISOTTO ALLA MILANESE)

4 tablespoons butter
1 small onion, finely chopped
2 tablespoons bone marrow
3 cups Arborio rice
½ cup dry white wine
6 cups boiling meat stock
⅛ teaspoon saffron, soaked in a little water
Salt and black pepper to taste
½ cup grated Parmesan cheese

Melt 2 tablespoons of the butter in a 3-quart saucepan, add onion and bone marrow and saute until onion is limp.

Add rice, stir gently with the onion and bone marrow and saute for a few minutes longer. Pour in wine and when it has evaporated, pour in one cup of stock. Stir constantly until stock has evaporated and pour in another cup. Continue to stir and add more stock as the previous addition evaporates and until rice is nearly cooked. Add the saffron and cook for another 2 or 3 minutes, stirring continually. Season with salt and pepper, and add remaining butter and cheese. Stir well and serve.

Serves 6

Cheese And Rice Omelette, Italian Style

(OMELETTE DI RISO)

8 eggs
Salt and black pepper to taste
3 tablespoons butter
¼ pound Mozzarella cheese, diced
2 ounces cooked ham, diced
1 cup warm boiled rice

Beat eggs lightly. Add salt and pepper to taste. Heat in a heavy saute pan and pour in eggs. Saute as you would an omelet.

Mix together the cheese, ham and rice. When the omelette is set but still moist, spread the rice mixture down the middle. Fold omelette over with a spatula. Continue cooking over low heat until omelette and rice are heated through.

Serves 4

Lightly Fried Eggs With Fontina Cheese

(UOVA FRITTE ALLA FONTINA)

8 slices bread
½ cup butter
8 slices Fontina cheese
8 anchovy fillets
8 eggs
Black pepper to taste

Preheat oven to 350° F.

Cut bread slices into rounds about 2½ inches in diameter. Melt half the butter and gently fry the rounds on one side only, until crisp.

Arrange rounds in a shallow, greased casserole, fried side up. Place a slice of Fontina cheese on each round. Place a half chopped anchovy fillet on each cheese slice. Sprinkle with pepper and place in oven long enough for cheese to melt, approximately 5 minutes.

Saute the eggs in the remaining butter and place one egg on each round. In the same pan, quickly fry the remaining anchovies until they dissolve into a paste. Spoon over the eggs and serve immediately.

Serves 4

Classic Polenta

(POLENTA)

6 cups salted water
1¾ cups fine cornmeal

Bring salted water to a boil and sprinkle the cornmeal in very slowly, stirring constantly with a wooden spoon. It is important that the cornmeal be added very slowly and that stirring is continuous to prevent lumping. Continue to stir polenta over low heat until the mixture starts to come away from the sides of the saucepan, 30 to 40 minutes.

Note:
Polenta may be spooned onto plates, or poured onto a platter to firm up and cut into squares. It may be used as a side dish with Beef in Barolo Wine, Ossobuco or Guinea Hen Forestiere. Cold polenta may be sliced and baked with cheese and tomatoes. It may be grilled, or cut into strips and fried.

Serves 4

Four-Cheese Polenta Timbale
(PASTICCIO DI POLENTA E FORMAGGI)

1 polenta recipe (see page 72).
⅓ pound Fontina cheese, thinly sliced
⅓ pound Mozzarella cheese, diced
¼ pound Gorgonzola cheese, diced
5 tablespoons butter
⅓ cup grated Parmesan cheese

Prepare polenta as recipe indicates. Pour polenta into a greased large dish and let cool. Cut into squares.

Preheat oven to 375° F.

Generously grease a baking dish. Place a layer of polenta squares on bottom of baking dish and cover with a layer of each of the cheeses, except the Parmesan cheese. Repeat the layers, ending with tree layers of polenta. Dot top layer of polenta with the butter and sprinkle with Parmesan cheese. Place in oven and bake for 10 to 15 minutes, or until cheese is melted and polenta is cooked through and lightly browned on top.

Serves 6

Polenta With Mushroom Sauce

(POLENTA AI FUNGHI)

1 Polenta recipe (see page 72)

Make Polenta according to recipe. When finished, pour into a large, shallow bowl. Pour the sauce on the polenta and sprinkle with Parmesan cheese.

SAUCE:

1 ounce dried porcini mushrooms, chopped
2 tablespoons olive oil
2 tablespoons butter
1 small onion, finely chopped
1 clove garlic
12 ounces fresh mushrooms, cleaned and sliced
3 ripe tomatoes, peeled, seeded and chopped
Salt and pepper to taste

Soak the dried mushrooms in warm water for 10 minutes. Set aside.

Meanwhile heat oil and butter in a saucepan, add the onion and garlic and saute until onion is limp. Discard garlic. Drain porcini mushrooms and add with the fresh ones to the onions and cook over medium-high heat for about 10 minutes. Do not burn the onion. Add tomatoes and simmer over low heat for 20 minutes. Season with salt and pepper.

Serves 6

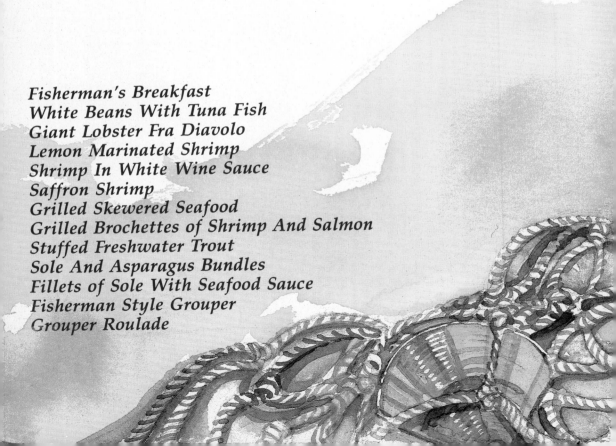

Fisherman's Breakfast
White Beans With Tuna Fish
Giant Lobster Fra Diavolo
Lemon Marinated Shrimp
Shrimp In White Wine Sauce
Saffron Shrimp
Grilled Skewered Seafood
Grilled Brochettes of Shrimp And Salmon
Stuffed Freshwater Trout
Sole And Asparagus Bundles
Fillets of Sole With Seafood Sauce
Fisherman Style Grouper
Grouper Roulade

Fish and Shellfish

Fisherman's Breakfast
(INSALATA MARINARA)

2 medium onions, cut into small wedges
6 ripe firm tomatoes, cut into small wedges
2 cucumbers, cut into wedges
4 boiled potatoes, peeled and cut into wedges
8 salted anchovies, well cleaned and boneless
1 pinch oregano
Salt to taste
2 tablespoons wine vinegar
⅓ cup olive oil
8 salted biscuits, or wedges of Italian bread
White wine to taste

Place all vegetables and anchovies in a large bowl. Mix the oregano, salt and vinegar in a smaller bowl. Slowly add the oil, mixing well. (This may be mixed in a food processor).

Pour sauce over the vegetables and toss well.

Moisten the biscuits, if using them, with white wine and water, and arrange decoratively around edges of salad. If using bread, do not moisten.

Serves 4

White Beans With Tuna Fish

(FAGIOLI AL TONNO)

1 pound Fagioli (giant white beans)
½ cup olive oil
1 clove garlic, crushed
6 large ripe tomatoes, peeled and chopped
Salt and black pepper to taste
12 ounces tuna fish in oil, drained and cut into pieces
2 or 3 sprigs of basil (chopped)

Soak beans in water, covered, overnight. Drain and cook in water covered until tender, about 1½ hours. Drain.

Heat oil in a large saute pan and saute garlic until brown. Discard garlic and add tomatoes. Add salt and pepper to taste and simmer over medium heat for 10 minutes. Stir in beans and pieces of tuna. Sprinkle with basil and more pepper if desired. Simmer for 10 more minutes over low heat and serve hot.

Serves 6

Giant Lobster Fra Diavolo

(ARAGOSTA FRA DIAVOLO)

1 (6-pound) lobster
4 tablespoons butter
4 tablespoons olive oil
2 cloves garlic, chopped
Salt to taste
1 pound peeled and chopped tomatoes, fresh or canned,
    drained
1 cup tomato puree
1 teaspoon oregano
1 teaspoon crushed red pepper
Rice or noodles

Cut lobster into pieces without removing shell. Heat butter and oil over medium heat and arrange lobster pieces evenly in pan. Saute until shells turn reddish. Add chopped garlic and salt. Cook for 2 minutes then add tomatoes. Cook for 5 minutes longer and add tomato puree. Simmer for 15 more minutes until sauce is reduced and thickened. Sprinkle with oregano and crushed pepper. Cook 5 minutes more and serve over rice or noodles.

Serves 6

Lemon Marinated Shrimp

(GAMBERI MARINATI AL LIMONE)

6 cups water
3 pounds fresh shrimp
1 tablespoon salt
½ cup lemon juice
½ cup cooking oil
3 tablespoons olive oil
2 tablespoons snipped parsley
Salt to taste
2 teaspoons drained capers

Bring water to a boil in a large saucepan. Add shrimp and salt and return to boil. Reduce heat and simmer for 1 to 3 minutes, or until shrimp turn pink. Drain. Cut any large shrimp in half, lengthwise.

Combine lemon juice, cooking oil, olive oil, parsley and salt and pour over shrimp. Toss to coat. Cover and refrigerate several hours or overnight, stirring occasionally.

To serve, drain shrimp and sprinkle with capers.

Serves 6

Shrimp in White Wine Sauce
(GAMBERI AL VINO BIANCO)

2 tablespoons olive oil
2 cloves garlic
1½ pounds shelled shrimp
1 teaspoon flour
½ cup dry white wine
1 tablespoon minced parsley
Salt and black pepper to taste
1 tablespoon butter

Place oil in heated saucepan and add garlic. Saute over medium
heat for two minutes and add the shrimp. Saute until shrimp turns
pink. Add flour and stir in thoroughly. Add wine and saute until
slightly thickened. Add parsley and salt and pepper. Add butter
and when it is well incorporated remove from heat and serve.

Serves 4

Saffron Shrimp
(GAMBERI ALLO ZAFFERANO)

2 tablespoons butter
¼ cup cooking oil
1 tablespoon chopped onion
1 clove garlic, minced
1½ pounds shrimp
¼ cup dry white wine
Pinch of saffron powder
¼ cup Pernod
¼ cup heavy cream
Salt and black pepper to taste
4 tablespoons cooked tomato sauce
1 tablespoon minced parsley

Heat saucepan and add butter and oil. Add onion and garlic and saute over medium heat until onions are limp. Add shrimp and saute until shrimp turns pink. Do not overcook. Add the wine, saffron, Pernod and the cream. Simmer 2 minutes and add salt and pepper. Remove shrimp and if necessary, reduce the Pernod and cream until sauce is thickened. Add tomato sauce and parsley. Heat until bubbly. Add the shrimp and heat again for 1 minute. Serve.

NOTE: Be careful not to overcook shrimp as they become tough with excessive cooking.

Serves 4

Grilled Skewered Seafood

(SPIEDINI ALLA MARINARA)

¼ cup olive oil
2 tablespoons fresh lemon juice
1 teaspoon chili pepper
Salt and pepper to taste
8 large shelled shrimp
8 small cleaned calamari (squid)
8 sea scallops
12 cherry tomatoes
8 squares green bell pepper

Mix together olive oil, lemon juice, chili pepper and salt and pepper. Add the seafood, mix well and marinate for about ½ hour.

Alternate seafood and vegetables on 4 (8-11") skewers. Grill for approximately 10 minutes, turning to brown on all sides. Serve hot.

Garnish with papaya, lemon slices or other fruits or vegetables.

Serves 4

Grilled Brochettes Of Shrimp And Salmon

(SPIEDINI DI GAMBERI E SALMONE)

MARINADE:
1 clove garlic, finely chopped
1 bunch chives, chopped
2 tablespoons chopped parsley
5 tablespoons olive oil
Juice of 2 lemons
Salt and pepper to taste

Prepare the marinade by mixing the garlic, chives, parsley, oil, lemon juice and salt and pepper.

BROCHETTES:
1 pound fresh salmon
4 slices lean bacon
18 shrimp

Cut salmon into 1½ inch cubes. Cut each slice of bacon into four pieces. Using 6 skewers, alternate the salmon, bacon and shrimp. Marinate for 3 or more hours.

Grill brochettes on all sides, basting from time to time with marinade. Do not overcook. Serve immediately.

Serves 6

Stuffed Freshwater Trout
(TROTE FARCITE)

6 trout, washed and cleaned
10 tablespoons soft bread crumbs
Salt and pepper to taste
4 to 5 sprigs parsley, finely chopped
Juice of 2 lemons
½ cup olive oil

Preheat oven to 350° F. Dry trout on paper toweling and set aside.

Combine bread crumbs, a bit of salt, a generous amount of ground pepper, the parsley and lemon juice. Mix well but lightly. Divide into 6 parts and stuff trout. Spread any remaining stuffing over fish.

Heat olive oil in a large saute pan. Add the trout in a single layer and cover the pan. Transfer to heated oven and bake about 20 minutes or until done. Do not overcook.

Serves 6

Sole And Asparagus Bundles

(ROLLATINE DI SOGLIOLA CON ASPARAGI)

1 pound fresh asparagus spears, peeled
1 tablespoon butter
6 fresh fillets of sole or other similar fish
Salt and black pepper to taste
4 tablespoons olive oil
1 clove garlic, mashed
1 medium onion, chopped
3 medium tomatoes, peeled, seeded and chopped
3 tablespoons chopped fresh basil

Cut asparagus into 6-inch lengths. Boil in water until tender, about 8 minutes. Drain on paper towels and set aside.

Heat butter in a saute pan and add fillets. Brown lightly on both sides, and sprinkle lightly with salt and pepper.

Divide asparagus into six small bundles and place them across each fillet. Roll up fillets and fasten with wooden pick.

Heat oil in a saucepan, add the garlic and chopped onion, and saute until onions are limp. Add tomatoes and simmer over low heat for about 15 minutes. Place the bundles in the sauce and cook for 8 to 10 minutes more, turning gently several times.

Place the fish bundles in a warm serving dish, pour sauce over them and sprinkle with basil. Serve hot.

Serves 6

Fillets Of Sole With Seafood Sauce

(FILETTI DI SOGLIOLA AI FRUTTI DI MARE)

4 tablespoons olive oil
1 anchovy fillet
4 fillets of sole
1 teaspoon chopped garlic
8 large shrimp
8 clams
2 whole calamari (squid), cleaned and cut into rings
3 cloves chopped garlic
1 cup dry white wine
1 cup fresh, peeled and chopped tomatoes
Salt and pepper to taste
1 tablespoon parsley

Preheat oven to 350° F.

In a skillet large enough to hold fillets, heat 2 tablespoons of the olive oil. Dry fillets on paper towels and saute in oil until golden. Remove from skillet, place in oven-proof casserole dish and keep warm.

In the same skillet, add the remaining olive oil, anchovy fillet and chopped garlic. Saute for several minutes. Add seafood and saute 5 more minutes. Add wine and tomatoes and continue cooking 10 minutes more, adding salt and pepper to taste. Add parsley. Pour the mixture on the fillets of sole and bake in preheated over for approximately 15 minutes. Serve hot with toasted, seasoned bread.

Serves 4

Fisherman Style Grouper

(CERNIA ALLA MARINARA)

4 tablespoons olive oil
3 cloves garlic, chopped
4 anchovy fillets
8 small grouper fillets or firm white fish fillets
2½ cups peeled and chopped tomatoes
Salt and black pepper to taste

Preheat oven to 350° F.

Pour olive oil into saute pan. When heated add garlic and saute lightly for one minute. Add tomatoes and anchovies and simmer for about 5 minutes.

Place fillets in a greased shallow baking dish and pour tomato sauce over them. Salt and pepper to taste. Bake in preheated oven for approximately 15 minutes or until fillets are cooked through. Be careful not to overcook.

Serves 4

Grouper Roulade
(INVOLTINI DI CERNIA)

4 pounds grouper fillets or firm white fish fillets
¼ pound (1 stick) butter, softened
2 cups dry bread crumbs
½ cup Parmesan cheese
1 teaspoon salt
1 tablespoon chopped parsley
1 small clove garlic, finely chopped
Boiled potatoes for garnish

Preheat oven to 350° F.

Dry grouper fillets on paper toweling. Combine half the butter with the bread, Parmesan cheese, salt, parsley and garlic. Divide the mixture evenly among the fillets. Roll each fillet as securely as possible around the stuffing and place in greased 10" x 10" baking pan. Dot with remaining butter. Bake in oven for 15 to 20 minutes or until fish is cooked through but not overdone.

Serve with a portion of the sauce in the pan. Garnish with boiled potatoes.

Serves 6

Chicken With Tomatoes And Peppers
Chicken Cacciatora
Chicken Breasts With Fresh Mangoes
Chicken With Marsala Sauce
Guinea Hens Forestiere
Country Style Guinea Fowl
Glazed Duck Puccini Style
Duckling In Orange Sauce
Turkey Breasts With Wine And Fresh Sage

Veal Scaloppine With Marsala Wine Sauce
Veal Scaloppine Alla Romana
Veal Chops Piquante
Veal Roulade With Lean Bacon
Tenderloins of Veal Riviera
Veal Chops In White Wine Sauce
Baked Veal Shank

Skewers of Beef Tenderloin Flambe
Meat Rissoles With Sage
Braised Beef In Barolo Wine
Meatballs And Peas In Fresh Tomato Sauce
Calf's Liver Venetian Style

Poultry and Meats

Chicken With Tomatoes And Peppers

(POLLO ALL'ABRUZZESE)

1 (3 to 3½) pound chicken
½ cup olive oil
1 small onion, chopped
Salt and pepper to taste
1 pound ripe tomatoes, peeled, seeded and chopped
2 large sweet bell peppers

Cut chicken into serving pieces. Heat oil in a heatproof casserole and saute the onion until limp. Add the pieces of chicken and saute gently, turning to brown all over. Season to taste with salt and pepper and add the tomatoes. Cover casserole and simmer gently for ½ hour.

Meanwhile, char the peppers over a high flame or under a broiler until skins blacken and blister. Place in a paper bag, seal and let stand for about 10 minutes. Remove from bag and peel off skins. Cut peppers into strips, discarding cores and seeds. Add the pepper strips to the casserole with the chicken and continue to simmer gently for about 15 minutes longer, or until chicken and peppers are cooked through and tender.

Serves 4

Chicken Cacciatora

(POLLO ALLA CACCIATORA)

6 tablespoons olive oil
1 onion, chopped
1 carrot, cut into julienne strips
2 stalks celery, cut into julienne strips
3 cloves garlic, chopped
1 (3 pound) chicken, cut into 8 pieces
1 cup dry white wine
2½ cups peeled, chopped tomatoes
1 cup sliced mushrooms
1½ cups consomme
Salt and Pepper to taste

Heat oil in a large saute pan. Add onion, carrot, celery and garlic. Saute lightly until onion is limp. Add the chicken pieces and, over medium high heat, saute until browned on both sides, about 10 minutes. Add wine and continue cooking until wine evaporates. Add tomatoes and mushrooms, and saute briefly. Add consomme and simmer slowly for about 35 minutes. Correct seasoning if necessary and serve.

Serves 4

Chicken Breasts With Fresh Mangoes

(PETTI DI POLLO AL MANGO)

6 chicken breasts
Salt and pepper to taste
Flour for dusting chicken
4 tablespoons butter or margarine
4 tablespoons chicken stock
2 mangoes
¼ cup heavy cream
4 tablespoons brandy
2 tablespoons mango chutney
1 tablespoon potato starch

Salt and pepper the chicken breasts and dust lightly with flour.

Heat the butter in a large saute pan with lid. Fry breasts on both sides until lightly browned, about 5 minutes. Add stock, cover with lid and simmer over low heat for 10 minutes more.

Meanwhile cut the mangoes in half, peel off skin and cut flesh from stone into thin slices. When breasts are cooked, remove from saute pan and keep warm. Place same pan over moderate heat and add heavy cream, brandy and chutney. Cool for a few minutes. Mix potato starch with a little of the sauce and add to skillet. Mix in thoroughly and cook over low heat until lightly thickened.

To serve, cut breast into slantwise slices and arrange on warm plates, alternating with slices of mango. Add some of the sauce to the chicken breast slices. Serve.

Serves 6

Chicken With Marsala Sauce

(POLLO AL MARSALA)

2 (3-pound) chickens
Salt and pepper to taste
All-purpose flour for dusting chicken
6 tablespoons olive oil
1 cup hot chicken broth
4 tablespoons butter
1 cup Marsala wine

Cut chicken into six to eight pieces. Sprinkle with salt and pepper. Dust lightly with flour.

Heat oil in large skillet. Brown chicken pieces on all sides over high heat. Lower heat, add broth and simmer gently until broth has evaporated and chicken is cooked through.

Transfer chicken to a heated serving dish and keep warm. Add butter to the cooking skillet and when melted add the Marsala. Stir over moderate heat until Marsala has been well mixed with the butter, and has been reduced to a slightly thickened sauce. Strain, pour over chicken and serve.

Serves 6

Guinea Hens Forestiere

(FARAONA ALLA FORESTIERA)

2 Guinea hens, approximately 2½ pounds each
Salt and pepper to taste
1 cup flour
4 tablespoons olive oil
4 tablespoons butter
1 sprig of thyme or 2 bay leaves
½ cup dry white wine
½ cup beef stock
6 small carrots, scraped
3 small zucchini, quartered
6 small onions
12 small mushrooms, cleaned
6 small potatoes, peeled
2 ounces goose liver
1 cup Madeira or Marsala wine
2 tablespoons chopped parsley

Heat oven to 350° F.

Cut Guinea hens into quarters. Remove all small bones. Rub with salt and pepper and dust lightly with flour. Save remaining flour.

Heat oil and all but 1 tablespoon of the butter in a large saute pan. Add hen pieces and brown on all sides. Add thyme or bay leaves and stir and cook for several minutes. Add wine and cook over high heat until evaporated. Add beef stock, reduce heat to low and simmer for 30 minutes longer. Skim surface during cooking if necessary.

Meanwhile place carrots, zucchini, onions, mushrooms and potatoes in an oven-proof casserole. Add a pinch of salt and remaining tablespoon of butter. Bake in preheated oven until crisp-cooked.

continued

Mix vegetables with the guinea hen pieces in saute pan. Remove from heat. Blend goose liver with Madeira or Marsala wine and pour over hen. Place in an oven-proof casserole. Sprinkle with chopped parsley and keep warm.

Raise oven heat to 425° F.

Make a dough with the remaining flour and a little water. Roll into a rope long enough to fit around casserole. Place lid on casserole and seal with the rope of dough as tightly as possible to prevent steam from escaping. Place casserole in preheated oven for approximately 10 minutes. Remove dough and lid immediately before serving, but be careful that steam does not burn your hands or face.

Serves 6

Country Style Guinea Fowl
(FARAONA ALLA CAMPAGNOLA)

1 guinea fowl
¼ cup olive oil
Salt and pepper to taste
3 tablespoons butter
2 medium onions, finely chopped
2 carrots, finely chopped
2 stalks celery, finely chopped
2 sprigs parsley, finely chopped
1 sprig rosemary, finely chopped
1 cup dry white wine
½ cup water
1 white truffle, sliced wafer thin (optional)

Preheat oven to 375° F. Singe surface of guinea fowl, if necessary, to remove fine hairs. Clean carefully and reserve liver.

Place guinea fowl in a roasting pan, pour olive oil over surface, add salt and pepper to taste. Roast in a 375° F. preheated oven for 35 to 45 minutes, or until tender, basting frequently to prevent dryness.

Place butter in a large pan, add all the vegetables and the herbs. Add the guinea fowl and the liver. Cover and braise on top of stove over low heat until vegetables are soft. Add the wine, season again to taste with salt and pepper and continue cooking until wine is reduced a little. Add ½ cup water and reduce over high heat. Put the vegetable, liver and liquid through a sieve, or process in food processor, to make a sauce. Return to pan, reheat, and, if necessary, reduce sauce to a rather thick consistency.

When the guinea fowl is tender, carve into serving pieces and arrange on a hot serving dish. Pour sauce over pieces and sprinkle with slices of truffle, optional.

Serves 3 or 4

Glazed Duck Puccini Style

(ANITRA GLASSATA ALLA PUCCINI)

4 duckling breast (approximately 2 pounds each)
2 tablespoons brown sugar
1 cup white wine
2 cups peach juice
1 cup consomme
Salt and pepper to taste
1 pound peaches, peeled, seeded and quartered or sliced

Preheat oven to 425° F.

Place duckling breasts in a roasting pan and roast in hot oven for about 30 minutes. Remove from pan and drain off fat. Return breasts to pan. Mix together the sugar, wine, peach juice, consomme and salt and pepper. Pour over the duck pieces. Cover pan with heavy aluminum foil, reduce oven temperature to 325° F. and bake 15 minutes longer.

Strain liquid from roasting pan into a large saucepan. Reduce over high heat until it is syrupy. Add the peaches and simmer just until peaches are partially cooked.

Serve a duck breast with some of the glazed peaches to each person.

Serves 4

Duckling In Orange Sauce

(ANATRA ALL'ARANCIA)

2 (4-pound) ducklings
4 tablespoons butter
2 carrots, coarsely chopped
1 large onion coarsely chopped
1 clove garlic
1 sprig thyme
2 tablespoons tomato paste
Salt and pepper to taste
1 cup water
1 cup dry white wine
7 oranges
⅓ cup sugar
2 tablespoons water
4 tablespoons vinegar
2 tablespoons guava jelly or orange marmalade

Preheat oven to 450° F.

Clean ducklings and remove wing tips and necks and other necessary parts. Melt butter in a roasting pan and the wings, neck and
other parts along with coarsely chopped carrots and onion, the garlic
and thyme. Place in oven and roast until golden brown. Remove
from oven, remove duck parts and vegetables and place over burner
on top of stove. Skim off fat and reserve.

Add tomato paste to pan and stir over medium heat for 2 minutes.
Sprinkle with salt, then add the water and wine. Heat to boiling
then simmer until liquid has been reduced to a quarter of original
amount. Skim surface as required.

Peel one of the oranges and cut rind into thin strips. Put rinds in a
pan with water to cover and heat to boiling for 3 minutes. Drain.
Squeeze juice from peeled orange and reserve. Peel remaining oranges and cut into segments with knife. Reserve.

continued

102

Preheat oven to 400° F.

Rub ducklings inside and out with salt and smear with reserved fat. Place in roasting pan and roast, breast side down, in preheated oven for approximately 10 minutes. Turn on back and cook for another 20 to 30 minutes, or to taste, basting frequently with liquid from first pan. When done, remove from oven and place on a platter. Drain off fat and reserve for other roasts.

Transfer any sauce remaining from first pan to the pan in which ducks were roasted. Heat to boiling, scraping any particles remaining in bottom of pan. Strain. Place in a saucepan with orange juice.

In a small saucepan, combine sugar with two tablespoons water. Heat until sugar becomes brown. Add vinegar and the guava jelly. Mix in well and heat to boiling. Add the orange strips and heat through. Add to the sauce.

Cut ducks in halves, lengthwise, and serve ½ per person with some of the sauce. Garnish with orange sections.

Serves 4

Turkey Breasts With Wine And Sage

(FILETTI DI TACCHINO AL VINO E SALVIA)

12 small slices of turkey breasts (about 2 pounds)
Salt and white pepper to taste
Flour for dusting turkey slices
1 tablespoon butter
½ cup dry white wine
12 fresh sage leaves

Salt and pepper turkey slices and dust lightly with flour. Melt butter in a large saute pan over medium high heat. Add turkey slices and brown lightly on each side. Increase heat to high and add white wine. Let wine reduce by half, then add sage leaves. Lower heat and simmer for 10 minutes, turning slices after 5 minutes. Serve with pan juices.

Serves 6

Veal Scaloppine With Marsala Wine Sauce

(SCALOPPINE DI VITELLO AL MARSALA)

1 pound thin slices of veal
Flour for dusting
4 tablespoons butter
¼ cup Marsala wine
2 tablespoons concentrated beef bouillon
Salt and pepper to taste

Dry veal scallops on paper towels, pound to even thinness and dust with flour.

Melt butter in a large saute pan, add veal slices and saute until lightly golden. Mix Marsala wine with beef bouillon and pour over veal. Simmer until wine is almost evaporated. Salt and pepper to taste. Serve veal slices with some of the liquid remaining in pan.

Serves 4

Veal Scaloppine Alla Romana

(SCALOPPINE DI VITELLO ALLA ROMANA)

8 thin slices of veal, 2 ounces each
Salt and pepper to taste
8 sage leaves
8 ham slices
Flour for dusting veal
6 tablespoons butter
¼ cup dry white wine
½ lemon
1 pound shelled or frozen peas
5 mint leaves, finely chopped
Pinch of sugar

Pound veal slices as thinly as possible and rub with salt and pepper
to taste. Place a sage leaf in center of each and top each with a ham
slice. Secure veal, sage and ham with a skewer. Dust with flour.

Heat 4 tablespoons butter in a large saute pan and brown veal for 2
minutes on ham side and 5 minutes on opposite side. Remove from
pan and keep warm.

Pour white wine and juice from the ½ lemon in saute pan and heat.
Scrape bottom of pan to loosen particles of drippings. Mix together
well and when it is bubbling pour over veal scaloppine and serve at
once. You may, if you wish, strain sauce before pouring over meat.

Heat remaining butter in a saucepan and add the peas, mint and
sugar. Stir until heated through and serve with the veal.

Serves 4

Veal Chops Piquante
(COSTOLETTE DI VITELLO IN SALSA PICCANTE)

6 veal cutlets
Salt and pepper to taste
Flour for dusting
4 tablespoons butter
3 anchovy fillets
2 gherkins
1 tablespoon capers
1 clove garlic
2 tablespoons chopped parsley
2 tablespoons vinegar

Rub veal chops with salt and pepper and dust lightly with flour. Heat butter in a large saute pan and add the veal chops. Cook over moderate heat but do not brown.

Meanwhile, chop anchovies, gherkins, capers and garlic and mix with parsley. Heat vinegar in a small skillet and add the chopped ingredients. Allow to cook for a few minutes and pour over the cutlets in saute pan. Continue sauteeing for a few minutes longer, basting with the vinegar mixture. Serve at once.

Serves 6

Veal Roulade With Lean Bacon

(ROLLATA DI VITELLO CON PANCETTA AFFUMICATA)

3 pounds tender veal meat cut into one slice
4 leeks, white part only, sliced crosswise
12 slices bacon
Salt and pepper to taste
½ cup olive oil
10 ounces mushrooms, chopped
4 ripe tomatoes, peeled, seeded and chopped
½ cup dry white wine

Pound the veal in one piece, as thinly as possible. Place leeks in boiling water in sauce pan and simmer for 5 minutes. Drain.

Line bacon on the veal and sprinkle with leeks. Season with salt and pepper to taste. Roll the meat into a neat roll tucking in ends. Tie with string at three or four intervals, and lengthwise, to secure the roll.

Heat olive oil in a large saute pan that can be placed in the oven, and add the roulade. Brown on all sides. Preheat oven to 350° F.

Lower the fire under the saute pan, add wine and when reduced by half, add the mushrooms and tomatoes. Simmer briefly and place the saute pan in the oven. Bake for 50 minutes, or until meat is tender. Remove meat from oven and remove strings. Strain the sauce. Slice the roll and arrange on a warm platter with the sauce.

NOTE: The roll will slice more easily if it is allowed to stand for 15 minutes.

Serves 6

Tenderloins Of Veal Riviera

(FILETTI DI VITELLO RIVIERA)

5 tablespoons butter
1 pound small potatoes, pared
4 fillets of veal tenderloin (½ pound each)
Salt and pepper to taste
Flour for dusting fillets
2 tablespoons olive oil
½ pound mushrooms, cut into thin slices
Juice of 1 lemon
2 scallions, finely chopped
1 tablespoon chopped parsley
2 ounces white truffle (optional) thinly sliced

Heat 2 tablespoons of the butter in a saute pan and saute potatoes until cooked and lightly browned on all sides. Or bake in a hot oven until browned and cooked through. Set aside and keep warm. Heat oven to 375° F.

Rub fillets with salt and pepper and dust with flour. Heat remaining butter and the oil in a large saute pan and brown fillets for 5 minutes on each side.

Butter a pan, preferably pyrex with a sealing lid, large enough to hold fillets. Sprinkle mushrooms with lemon juice. Spread half of mushrooms evenly on bottom. Sprinkle with salt to taste and spread chopped scallions and parsley over them Arrange fillets on top and surround with potatoes. Top with remaining mushrooms and the truffles if you are using them and cover. Bake for 15 minutes. Remove from oven and serve at once.

Serves 4

Veal Chops In White Wine Sauce

(COSTOLETTE DI VITELLO AL VINO BIANCO)

4 veal chops with bones attached
Salt and pepper to taste
Flour for dusting chops
2 tablespoons olive oil
1 cup dry white wine
2 cloves garlic, chopped
4 bay leaves

Dry veal chops on paper towels and sprinkle with salt and pepper.
Let sit for approximately ½ hour.

Coat chops lightly with the flour. Heat olive oil in a large skillet and
add the chops. Brown chops lightly on both sides. Add the wine,
garlic and bay leaves. Simmer for several minutes until wine has
been reduced to approximately ⅓ cup. Serve with some of the wine
sauce and garnish with buttered peas, French-fried potatoes and
steamed carrots.

Serves 4

Baked Veal Shank

(STINCO DI VITELLO AL FORNO)

1 (4 to 5 pound) veal shank, cut crosswise into four pieces
Salt and pepper to taste
Flour for dusting
½ cup olive oil
½ cup dry white wine
1 to 2 cups consomme
Rosemary to taste
Fresh sage to taste
Chopped parsley to taste
3 cloves garlic, chopped
4 medium potatoes, quartered
8 small onions
2 hearts of celery, sliced crosswise
4 tomatoes, peeled, seeded and halved

Preheat oven to 325° F.

Season the veal shank pieces with salt and pepper and dust with flour. Heat olive oil in a large, deep skillet and, over high heat, brown the shank pieces until golden brown. Add the white wine and continue cooking until wine has evaporated.

Place shanks in a casserole and add one cup of consomme. Cover and bake for one hour, adding more consomme if needed. Add the herbs, garlic and the vegetables, except the tomatoes, and bake, covered, for one hour or more, until the meat is tender and vegetables are cooked.

Grill or broil the tomato halves and serve with the veal shanks and the cooked vegetables and sauce from the casserole.

Serves 4

Skewers Of Beef Tenderloin Flambe

(SPIEDINI DI FILETTO FLAMBE)

1½ pounds beef tenderloin
4 bay leaves, halved
Salt and black pepper to taste
Paprika to taste
4 tablespoons olive oil
1 clove garlic, chopped
4½ ounces lean salt pork, cut into 1-inch cubes
2 tablespoons brandy

Trim tenderloin of any skin and fat, then cut into 1-inch cubes.

Mix together the bay leaves, salt and pepper, paprika, 2 tablespoons olive oil, and garlic. Add the tenderloin cubes, mix well and marinate for several hours. Stir mixture occasionally.

Alternate, on four skewers, the diced beef, salt pork and bay leaves. Heat remaining 2 tablespoons olive oil in a saute pan and saute skewers until brown, about ten minutes. Remove from heat, place on a pan and sprinkle with cognac. Ignite and serve while still blazing. Careful!
Serves 4

Meat Rissoles With Sage

(POLPETTINE ALLA SALVIA)

2 cups ground lean beef
8 sage leaves, finely chopped
8 tablespoons butter
2 egg yolks
3 tablespoons Parmesan cheese
Salt and pepper to taste
Flour for dusting
¼ cup Marsala wine

Mix together the beef, sage, 2 tablespoons butter, egg yolks and grated Parmesan cheese. Add salt and pepper to taste.

With floured hands, break off pieces of mixture and shape into small rissoles, or "patties" about 1 inch around and ½ inch thick. Dust with flour.

Melt remaining butter in a saute pan and add the rissoles. Brown on both sides, about 6 to 7 minutes. Add Marsala wine and reduce it to a glaze. Serve with some of the cooking juices.

Serves 4

Braised Beef In Barolo Wine

(BRASATO AL BAROLO)

2½ pounds lean beef
1 bay leaf
1 clove garlic, chopped
Salt and pepper to taste
¼ teaspoon grated nutmeg
6 cloves
2 cups Barolo or other red wine
3 tablespoons olive oil
2 tablespoons butter
1 medium onion, diced
1 medium carrot, diced
1 stalk celery, diced
2 ounces tomato paste

Allow time for meat to marinate, at least 8 hours. Cut meat into 6 pieces of equal size. Dry on paper towels, place in a bowl, and set aside. Mix together the bay leaf, garlic, salt and pepper, nutmeg and cloves. Add wine and mix. Pour over the meat and let marinate in a cool place, covered, for at least 8 hours, or overnight, turning meat occasionally.

Heat olive oil at low temperature and add butter. Saute the onion, carrot and celery until onion is limp but not brown. Add tomato paste, stir well, and cook sauce for a few minutes. Remove from pan and set aside. Remove meat from marinade, and pat dry on paper towels. Add meat to the saute pan and brown on both sides over moderate heat. Return the vegetables to the pan, strain 1 cup of the marinade over meat, cover pan and simmer slowly for 2 hours, or until meat is very tender. Add more marinade if needed during the simmering process. Mixture should not be dry. Remove meat from pan and reduce liquid in pan until it is of sauce consistency. Serve meat with some of the sauce.

Serves 6

Meatballs And Peas In Fresh Tomato Sauce

(POLPETTE DI CARNE AL POMODORO CON PISELLI)

5 slices solid white bread
1 cup milk
1½ pounds lean ground beef
½ cup grated Parmesan cheese
1 clove garlic, finely chopped
Salt and pepper to taste
2 eggs, slightly beaten
Flour for dusting
Enough oil for deep frying
2 tablespoons olive oil
1 onion, sliced
1½ pounds ripe tomatoes, peeled, seeded and chopped
1 teaspoon tomato paste, diluted in ¼ cup hot water
1 pound green peas, fresh or frozen

Soak bread in the milk and squeeze out as much of milk as possible.

In a bowl, combine the bread, meat, cheese, garlic, salt and pepper and eggs. Mix thoroughly. Break off small pieces of mixture and form into small, round balls. Roll them lightly in flour.

Heat oil in deep fryer to 350° F. Add the meatballs and deep fry until golden brown. Drain on paper toweling and keep warm.

In a saucepan heat the olive oil and saute the sliced onion until limp. Add the tomatoes and the diluted tomato paste. Stir and mix well and simmer over low heat for about 30 minutes. Drop meatballs into the tomato sauce with the peas and simmer gently for 10 more minutes.

Serves 6

Calf's Liver, Venetian Style

(FEGATO ALLA VENEZIANA)

6 tablespoons olive oil
1 pound onions, sliced
1¼ pounds calf's liver, sliced into strips
Salt and pepper to taste
Flour for dusting liver
4 tablespoons white wine
1 tablespoon finely chopped parsley

Heat olive oil in saute pan and add onions. Saute until limp but not brown. Remove onions from pan and keep warm.

Salt and pepper the liver and dust with flour. Saute the liver in the same pan, turning frequently for 3 to 4 minutes. Return the onions to the pan, season with salt and pepper again if necessary and add white wine. Simmer until wine is reduced to about half. Sprinkle with parsley and serve.

Serves 6

Fresh Pears In Chianti Wine Sauce
Sweet Words
Tiramisu
Strawberries With Wine Vinegar
Fresh Fruit Salad With Maraschino Liquor
Pineapple With Cola Syrup
Italian Fruit Fritters
Chilled Gianduia Pudding
Crepes Flamed With Orange Sauce
Amaretto Souffle
Fresh Fruit Torte, Italian Style
Baba Rum Cakes
Sicilian Cannoli
Zabaione
Almond Macaroons

Desserts

Fresh Pears In Chianti Wine Sauce

(PERE AL CHIANTI)

6 winter pears
2 cups granulated sugar
Rind of ½ lemon
1 cinnamon stick
2 tablespoons vanilla sugar
1 bottle Chianti wine

Peel pears, leaving the stems attached and place then in a pan, stem side up. Mix together half the sugar, lemon rind, cinnamon, vanilla and wine. Pour over pears and bring to a boil. Lower heat and simmer until pears are cooked but still firm, about 30 minutes. Remove pears and cool.

Add remaining sugar to the wine mixture and boil over high heat until liquid is reduced to a syrup, about 20 minutes. Pour syrup over the pears and chill in refrigerator. Serve cold with some of the syrup.

Serves 6

Sweet Words

(CHIACCHIERE)

1¾ cups all-purpose flour
2 tablespoons butter
4 teaspoons granulated sugar
1 pinch of salt
2 eggs
2½ tablespoons white wine
Grated rind of ½ lemon
Oil for deep frying
Confectioner's sugar

Sift flour into a bowl and rub in the butter. Add sugar, salt, eggs, lemon rind and white wine. Work to a rather stiff, but pliable dough. Knead well and let sit in a cool place for 1 hour, covered with a wet cloth.

Roll out dough as thinly as possible and cut into 3 by 4½ inch rectangles. Make three lengthwise cuts on each rectangle, leaving ½ inch uncut at each end. The effect should be of 4 thin strips joined at each end. Intertwine strips to look like knots.

Preheat oil in deep fryer to 375° F. Fry the strips, two or three at a time, until puffed and golden. Drain on paper towels and when cool, sprinkle with sifted confectioner's sugar. May be served alone, with fruit or with a cold mousse.

Serves 4

Tiramisu

(TIRAMISU)

1 egg yolk
1 tablespoon sugar
1 tablespoon vanilla sugar
9 ounces Mascarpone cheese
¾ cup strong black coffee
1 tablespoon Kahlua or other coffee liqueur
12 lady fingers
2 tablespoons unsweetened cocoa powder

Place the egg and sugars in a mixing bowl and beat until creamy. Fold in Mascarpone to form a rich cream.

Place the coffee in a bowl and add the Kahlua. Dip the lady fingers in the coffee mixture, letting them absorb enough coffee, while remaining firm.

Place the ladyfingers in a single layer and cover with the Mascarpone mixture. Refrigerate until chilled and set (4 hours or overnight). Dust with the cocoa powder and serve.

Serves 4

Strawberries With Wine Vinegar

(FRAGOLE ALL' ACETO DI VINO)

1 quart strawberries
¼ cup sugar
¼ cup white wine vinegar
Whipped cream (optional)
Sprig of fresh mint

Clean strawberries. Crush 1 cup of strawberries and combine with sugar and vinegar, stirring to dissolve sugar. Pour over whole strawberries and stir gently to mix.

Cover and refrigerate for 1 to 2 hours before serving. Divide into six portions and serve with whipped cream in crystal goblet with sprig of mint.

Serves 6

Fresh Fruit Salad With Maraschino Liqueur

(MACEDONIA DI FRUTTA AL MARASCHINO)

2 apples
2 pears
2 peaches
1 medium pineapple
2 bananas
2 oranges
Juice of 1 lemon
Sugar to taste
2 ounces Maraschino Liqueur
2 tablespoons chopped hazelnuts

Peel and core fruit and cut into dice or slices. Add lemon juice, sugar and liquor. Mix well. Chill and serve in stemmed glasses. Sprinkle with chopped hazelnuts.

Serves 6

Pineapple With Cola Syrup

(ANANAS IN COLA)

8 slices ripe fresh pineapple, ⅓-inch thick
1 lemon peel
1 cup Coca-Cola®
4 tablespoons sugar
3 ounces light rum
1 cup heavy cream, whipped

Marinate pineapple slices with lemon peel in the cola for 2 hours.

Heat a saute pan and add sugar. When sugar begins to brown, add one cup of the cola marinate to the pineapple rings. Add rum and simmer for 5 to 8 minutes, until syrup is reduced by half.

Serve pineapple slices hot with a dollop of whipped cream.

Serves 4

Italian Fruit Fritters

(FRITTELLE DI FRUTTA)

1 cup all purpose flour
½ cup granulated sugar
1¼ teaspoon baking powder
⅛ teaspoon salt
2 egg yolks, beaten
½ cup milk
2 egg whites
2 medium apples
2 firm medium pears
2 cups strawberries
Oil for deep frying
Powdered sugar

Mix together the flour, granulated sugar, baking powder and salt. Set aside.

Combine egg yolks and milk and stir into the flour mixture. Beat egg whites until stiff peaks form and fold into mixture. Cover bowl and let sit for about 1 hour.

Meanwhile, peel and core apples and pears and slice crosswise into ¼-inch rings. Clean strawberries.

Heat oil in deep frying pan until it reaches a temperature of 375° F. Dip fruit into batter, one piece at a time, and fry in the hot oil for 2 to 3 minutes, or until golden. Sprinkle with powdered sugar and serve warm.

Serves 4

Chilled Gianduia Pudding

(BUDINO DI GIANDUIA)

1 egg
2 egg yolks
½ cup sugar
2½ squares bitter chocolate, grated
5 tablespoons butter
½ cup hazelnuts, lightly roasted and chopped
½ pound plain cookies, crushed
Butter for greasing pan
1 cup whipping cream, whipped

Beat the whole egg and yolks with the sugar until very light and fluffy. Add grated chocolate.

Melt butter in the top of a double broiler, over simmering water, and add the egg mixture. With a whisk, or a portable electric beater, beat mixture constantly until thickened. Fold in nuts and crushed cookies.

Line a rectangular cake pan with wax paper and grease with butter. Spoon in the mixture which should reach the top of the pan. Smooth top. Cool, then chill in the refrigerator until firm, four hours or overnight. Turn out on a platter and cut into slices. Serve with whipped cream.

Serves 6

Crepes Flamed With Orange Sauce

(CREPES SUZETTE)

½ cup all-purpose flour
Pinch of salt
1 tablespoon sugar
1 tablespoon grated orange peel
Dash of cinnamon
1½ cups milk
3 eggs
Melted butter (to coat) crepe pan
Orange sauce, recipe below

In an electric mixer, mix together all ingredients, except eggs and orange sauce, until a batter is formed. Add eggs, one at a time, making sure each egg is well incorporated before adding the next. Beat 4 to 5 minutes to form a smooth, thin batter. Refrigerate for two hours before making crepes.

To make crepes, heat a 6" non-stick frying or crepe pan. Brush with butter. When pan is hot, pour about ¼ cup batter into pan, or just enough batter to form a thin layer. Tilt pan as required to spread batter evenly. Heat briefly, and with a plastic spatula, turn crepe to cook on other side. Each crepe should take only a few seconds to cook. Crepes are done when lightly golden on each side. Makes 18 crepes. These may be made ahead and frozen with squares of foil between each crepe.

Heat the sauce, recipe below, and add crepes which have been folded into quarters. Cook until sauce and crepes are warmed through. Add the brandy and Grand marnier, flambe and serve.

continued

For the Orange Sauce:

Juice of three oranges
3 tablespoons sugar
Grated peel from one lemon
1 cinnamon stick
1 tablespoon sweet butter
2 tablespoons brandy
2 tablespoons Grand Marnier

Mix together all ingredients except brandy and Grand Marnier. Place in a 12-inch frying pan or flambe pan and bring to a boil. Simmer for 5 to 6 minutes and proceed as described above.

Serves 6

129

Amaretto Souffle

(AMARETTO SOUFFLE)

SOUFFLE:
1 pint (2 cups) milk
½ cup sugar
Pinch of salt
1 stick (4 ounces) butter
½ cup flour
8 large egg yolks
2 ounces Amaretto liqueur
8 large egg whites
Amaretto sauce (recipe below)

Heat oven to 300° F.

In a saucepan bring milk, sugar and salt to boil. Remove from heat.

In another saucepan, melt butter. Add flour and stir well. Slowly add the milk mixture, stirring constantly until thickened. Cover pan and cool slightly.

With a whisk, add the egg yolks, one at a time, mixing well after each addition.

Beat egg whites until they form stiff peaks. Fold egg whites into the egg yolk mixture stir in Amaretto and place in a greased and floured souffle dish. Place dish in a larger pan and fill, half-way up sides of souffle dish, with hot water. Bake for approximately 45 minutes or until souffle has puffed and browned on top. Serve immediately with Amaretto custard sauce, recipe below.

continued

AMARETTO CUSTARD SAUCE:

2 cups milk
1 slice lemon peel
1 cinnamon stick
2 egg yolks
2 tablespoons flour
4 tablespoons granulated sugar
1 to 2 ounces Amaretto liqueur
½ teaspoon vanilla

In a saucepan, bring milk to boil with lemon peel and cinnamon stick. When milk has reached boiling point remove from heat and remove the lemon peel and cinnamon stick.

Meanwhile mix together egg yolks, flour and sugar. Add some of the scalded milk to egg yolk mixture and whisk well. Return egg yolk mixture to the remaining milk in saucepan and place over simmering water on stove. Continue to stir with whisk until sauce has lightly thickened, for about 3 minutes. Add Amaretto and vanilla. Serve sauce hot or cold with souffle.

Serves 4

Fresh Fruit Torte, Italian Style

(TORTA CASSATA)

SPONGE CAKE:

6 eggs, separated
1½ cups sugar
1½ cups all-purpose flour
1 teaspoon baking powder
½ cup orange juice
1 teaspoon vanilla

To prepare sponge cake, preheat oven to 350° F. In an electric mixer, beat egg yolks until light yellow. Add sugar and beat until light and fluffy. Mix together the flour and baking powder. Mix together orange juice and vanilla. Alternately fold in the flour mixture and orange juice mixture, ending with flour.

Beat egg whites until firm peaks form. Fold into cake mixture. Pour into greased and floured springform pan and bake in oven for about 30 minutes, or until a tester comes out clean. Cool before removing from springform pan. Let cool completely before splitting and filling.

When sponge cake is cool, split into 3 even layers. Spread ⅓ of filling on bottom layer, top with another layer, and spread with another third of filling. Cover with top layer and spread remaining filling. Decorate with candied fruit if desired.

continued

FILLING:

8 ounces (1 cup) Ricotta cheese
½ cup sugar
1 teaspoon grated lemon rind
½ teaspoon vanilla
Dash of cinnamon
1 pint fresh strawberries, diced
2 kiwis, diced
½ cup blueberries

To make filling, mix together Ricotta cheese, sugar, lemon rind, vanilla, cinnamon and fruits.

Serves 12 to 16

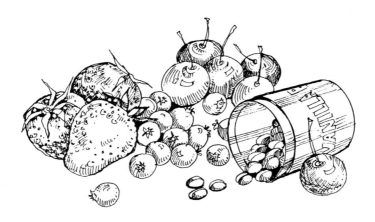

Baba Rum Cakes

(BABA AL RUM)

CAKE:
6 or more baba molds*, 2½ inches in diameter and 2 inches high
1½ cups all purpose flour
4 eggs
2 tablespoons sugar
Pinch salt
2 tablespoons butter, melted
2 drops lemon extract
1 teaspoon baking powder
Rum Syrup (recipe below)

Preheat oven to 350° F.

Place all the above ingredients, except rum syrup, in a food processor and pulse, on and off, until mixture is well mixed and soft. Add more milk if necessary. Remove from food processor and knead for several minutes.

Grease molds and fill each ¾ full with dough. Bake approximately 30 minutes, until babas have risen about ½ inch above molds and top is brown. Cool slightly and remove from molds. Cool completely before soaking with rum syrup, recipe below.

continued

*May substitute cupcake pans

RUM SYRUP:

½ cup sugar
1 slice lemon peel
2 cloves
1 cinnamon stick
½ cup water
6 ounces dark Jamaican rum

In a saucepan, mix together all above ingredients except rum. Bring to a boil and reduce by half. Remove lemon peel, cloves and cinnamon stick. Add rum. Dunk babas into rum syrup and soak through until all syrup is absorbed. These will keep, refrigerated, for several days.

May be served, if desired, with creme anglaise and a Maraschino cherry.

Serves 6

*May substitute cupcake pans

Sicilian Cannoli

(CANNOLI ALLA SICILIANA)

PASTRY:
1¼ cups all purpose flour
¼ cup sugar
1 egg
¼ cup butter, softened
¼ cup Marsala wine
1 teaspoon coffee powder
½ teaspoon vanilla
Oil for deep frying
12 metal cannoli shells
1 egg yolk for binding pastry
Candied cherries or chopped sweet chocolate
   (for decoration)

In a food processor mix all pastry ingredients, except oil, and process until a firm ball is formed. Add more flour if required. Knead in food processor for several seconds, or by hand for several minutes until dough is smooth. Let rest, covered with a napkin or bowl, for ½ hour.

On a floured board, roll out the pastry dough until thin. Cut into disks with a round pastry cutter (7 cm radius) about 3 inches. Roll disks around metal cannoli shells, pinching edges together and binding with a brushing of egg yolk.

Heat oil in deep fryer to a temperature of 375° F. Fry shells until browned. Place on paper towels to drain. Remove from metal shells and cool. Just before serving, stuff with filling, instructions below, decorating ends with candied cherries or chopped sweet chocolate.

continued

FILLING:

2 cups Ricotta
1 cup sugar
¼ cup chopped hazelnuts
½ cup chocolate chips
½ teaspoon vanilla
¼ cup chopped candied orange
Dash of orange and lemon extract

Mix Ricotta with sugar until well combined. Add remaining ingredients and mix thoroughly. Mixture should be soft but spoonable. Refrigerate to firm up, if too soft.

Makes 12 cannoli

Zabaione

(ZABAIONE)

6 egg yolks
8 tablespoons sugar
5 ounces Marsala wine

In the top of a double broiler mix together the egg yolks and sugar with a whisk until sugar is dissolved. Add Marsala wine. Place double boiler over barely simmering water and beat with a whisk or with a portable electric beater, beating constantly for about 20 minutes until a thick cream is formed. If you use an electric beater, the cream will form faster.

Serve warm, alone or over fresh berries.

Serves 6

Almond Macaroons

(AMARETTI ALLE MANDORLE)

1 pound almond paste
Pinch of cinnamon
½ teaspoon vanilla
8 egg whites
1 cup ground almonds

Preheat oven to 275° F.

Mix almond paste with cinnamon and vanilla and two egg whites.
Beat remaining egg whites until they form firm peaks. Quickly add
to almond paste mixture. This operation must be performed quickly so that egg whites will not become runny. Mix in ground
almonds.

Shape into small balls, about 1½ inches in diameter. Line a baking
sheet with wax paper. Place balls on wax paper and flatten slightly
to reduce height to half. Bake cookies for 1½ hours or until they
are dry and crispy.

Serves 6

Ships of the Costa Fleet

CarlaCosta   *Danae*

CostaRiviera   *EnricoCosta*

Daphne   *EugenioCosta*

CostaMarina

Costa Cruises, Inc. is headquartered in Miami, Florida with its parent company, Costa Crociere, based in Genoa, Italy. The company currently operates six ships, with routes in the Eastern and Western Caribbean, Alaska, Mediterranean and worldwide.

In July 1990, Costa will introduce the CostaMarina to its fleet. An additional ship, presently under construction and as yet unnamed, will be introduced in 1991.

For additional information, contact your travel agent or write to:
Costa Cruises, Inc./CB, 80 S.W. 8th Street, Miami, Florida, 33130-3097.

Index